VOTERS' VERDICTS

Constitutionalism and Democracy

GREGG IVERS AND
KEVIN T. MCGUIRE,
EDITORS

Voters' Verdicts

CITIZENS, CAMPAIGNS, AND INSTITUTIONS IN STATE SUPREME COURT ELECTIONS

Chris W. Bonneau and
Damon M. Cann

UNIVERSITY OF VIRGINIA PRESS
CHARLOTTESVILLE AND LONDON

University of Virginia Press

Printed in the United States of America on acid-free paper

First published 2015
9 8 7 6 5 4 3 2 1

LIBRARY OF CONGRESS CATALOGING-IN-PUBLICATION DATA
Bonneau, Chris W., author.
Voters' verdicts : citizens, campaigns, and institutions in state supreme court elections / Chris W. Bonneau and Damon M. Cann.
pages cm. — (Constitutionalism and democracy)
Includes bibliographical references and index.
ISBN 978-0-8139-3759-5 (cloth : alk. paper) — ISBN 978-0-8139-3760-1 (e-book)
1. Judges—United States—States—Election. 2. Courts of last resort—United States—States—Election. 3. Courts—United States—States—Election. 4. Courts of last resort—United States—States. 5. Voting—United States. 6. Elections. I. Cann, Damon M., 1976– author. II. Title.
KF8776.B66 2015
324.973—dc23

2014034590

To Heather Rice, Robinson J. Rice-Bonneau,
Boss Rice-Bonneau, & Izzo Rice-Bonneau,
who continue, without fail, to cast their votes
for me. —**CWB**

To Clair, Cambria, Ian, Colton, and Bradley, who
have faithfully retained me as a husband and
father even though I may not make a parental
nominating commission's top 3 list. —**DMC**

CONTENTS

ACKNOWLEDGMENTS

As with all long-term projects, we (collectively and individually) have racked up a lot of debts. Collectively, this work has benefited from the comments and suggestions of numerous colleagues: Melinda Gann Hall, Bobbi Herzberg, Mark Hurwitz, Mike MacKuen, Randy Simmons, Walt Stone, and Sarah Treul. We also presented portions of this work at UC–Davis and UNC–Chapel Hill and greatly benefited from comments from seminar participants there. Thanks to Todd Curry for sharing his data on which states denote incumbency on the ballot, which we used in chapter 4. We are appreciative of Larry Aspin for sharing his data on the 2012 retention elections that we used in chapter 5. An earlier version of chapter 2 and part of chapter 3 was published in *Political Behavior*, and the referees there (and at other journals) helped strengthen that analysis. We also acknowledge Jeremy Pope, Quin Monson, and David Barker, who helped to coordinate the swapping of questions across modules on the 2010 Cooperative Congressional Election Study (CCES) that allowed us to ask judicial vote choice questions of more respondents, and Steve Ansolabehere, who supported our request to put judicial vote choice on the 2012 CCES common content. Finally, portions of this project were funded by the Milton Merrill endowment in Utah State University's Political Science Department, which supported our acquisition of shares of the CCES in 2010 and 2012, and the Richard D. and Mary Jane Edwards Endowment Publication Fund at the Dietrich School of Arts and Sciences at the University of Pittsburgh, which funded the composition of the index.

Our editor, Dick Holway, and the staff at UVA Press have been extremely helpful, thorough, and professional throughout the project. The book publication process can be a bit onerous; working with UVA was truly pleasurable.

Bonneau's biggest intellectual and professional debt is to Melinda Gann Hall, who has been a fantastic role model for him over the past sixteen years. Everyone should be so fortunate to have such a caring and generous advisor. He is also grateful for the encouragement, support, and friendship of Kris Kanthak, George Krause, and Jon Woon, which has greatly improved the quality of this book. David Klinowski provided helpful research assistance for the conclusion. The faculty at Utah State were always very welcoming and generous with their time (and their students) in my trips out there. As always, Heather Rice has been an invaluable source of patience, strength, and good humor throughout the project.

Cann would like to thank his senior research seminar students from spring 2010 and spring 2012, who helped craft some of the questions that appeared on the CCES. He also thanks Andy Pierucci for helpful research assistance on the experiments in chapter 4. Finally, thanks are due to my USU colleagues, especially Greg Goelzhauser, Bobbi Herzberg, Michael Lyons, Randy Simmons, and the USU Political Economy Lunch Group, who offered helpful comments on life and scholarship. Extra thanks are due to Michael Lyons, Bobbi Herzberg, Kristen Dawson, and Lauren Fairbanks, who have allowed me to use their class time to recruit research subjects.

Finally, this collaboration is evidence that you never know where or when you are going to meet smart people with similar ideas. Specifically, we began talking about our common research interests at a job interview that did not have a positive result. We began emailing and exchanging comments on each other's work soon thereafter and eventually began writing together. Sometimes success can be born from failure.

VOTERS' VERDICTS

INTRODUCTION: THE LANDSCAPE OF JUDICIAL ELECTIONS

My name ID hovers between slim and none, and voters know far more about their American Idol judges than their Supreme Court judges. The crass bottom line is that you spend 99 percent of your time raising a colossal fortune that you then use to bombard voters in hopes of branding your name onto a tiny crevice in their short-term memory for a few fleeting moments.

—Texas Supreme Court justice Don Willett, "An Elected Judge Speaks Out against Judicial Elections"

Judicial elections have been described by critics as a failed experiment (O'Connor and McGregor 2012), "economically inefficient" (Chertoff 2010, 48), a "real and increasing threat to . . . fair and impartial courts" (O'Connor and McGregor 2012, 1742), "'wild,' 'crazy,' 'raucous,' 'radical,' 'nightmarish'" (Pozen 2008, 307), and dominated by "special-interest spending and politics on courts" (Bannon et al. 2013, 27). Indeed, some have even argued that "*unqualified voters* may now seem especially likely to make bad choices because a race to the bottom in judicial campaign tactics will lead them to pick politically appealing yet *lower-quality candidates*" (Pozen 2008, 304), and electing judges can lead to the death of criminal defendants (Brandenburg 2014).

As the nature of these races has been changing, they have drawn more attention from interest groups, the media, policymakers, and scholars. It is fair to say that over the past ten years, there has been an explosion of scholarship on judicial elections (for field essays on the current state of literature, see Bonneau 2012 and Gill 2013). Much of the debate has been about the desirability of electing judges as well as how well these elections actually function.

At the heart of judicial elections are the voters. Yet, although we have learned a great deal about the nature of these elections from prior work, we know relatively little about how voters behave in these elections. What factors determine participation? Or vote choice? What information is useful for voters to have? What information is extraneous? These questions go to the heart of judicial elections as efficacious mechanisms to promote accountability and ensure that judges are faithfully discharging their duties. This book offers a theoretical framework for understanding citizens' behavior in judicial elections by integrating individual-level factors with institutional and campaign-based explanations in a comprehensive analysis for understanding participation and vote choice in judicial elections. Without this, we cannot ascertain the determinants of the behavior of individual voters. Moreover, by combining race-level variables (such as quality challengers, campaign spending, etc.) with individual-level survey data, we will be able to explore important variations among races within a state, as well as races between states.

In this book, we use a combination of survey data and experiments to answer fundamental but unanswered questions about the decisions of individual voters in state supreme court elections. We primarily examine the influence of ballot cues on voters. Specifically, we compare political participation and vote choice between states (1) that provide candidates' partisan identification on the ballot and those that do not, and (2) that denote which candidate is the incumbent on the ballot and those that do not. In order to answer these questions, we need to study an office that has variation on both partisan identification and incumbency on the ballot. Fortunately, state supreme courts provide exactly such an environment. Indeed, state supreme courts have three forms of elections by which judges are selected: competitive partisan elections (partisan affiliation of candidates on the ballot), competitive nonpartisan elections (no partisan affiliation of candidates on the ballot), and noncompetitive retention elections (where judges are simply subjected to a yes/no vote on whether they should remain in office). This allows us to isolate the effect of ballot type, holding the office constant. Additionally, some states denote which candidate is the incumbent on the ballot, while other states do not provide voters with this information. This institutional variation will allow us to ascertain the true effect of incumbency on vote choice through the use of both experimental and observational data.

In the remainder of the introduction, we lay the groundwork for our analysis. We briefly discuss the characteristics of judicial selection systems, discuss recent changes to the legal landscape of these elections (changes that have or had the potential to fundamentally alter the nature of these elections), and summarize developments in judicial elections over the past decade.

Methods of Selection and Their Importance

By now, most people are aware that states select their judges in various manners. Here, we briefly recap these different methods of selection; for an excellent history of state judicial selection in the United States, see Shugerman (2012). Even within these broad categories, there are variations across the states in the way they select judges, and even variation within states: some states, like Florida and New York, use different methods of selection for different levels of court, and Kansas and Arizona have different methods of selection within the *same* level of court (trial court).

Partisan Elections. In seven states, judges are nominated by political parties in partisan primaries and then run in a general election with their political party affiliation noted on the ballot. These elections are similar to elections to the vast majority of statewide offices in this regard. Existing empirical literature (e.g., Bonneau and Hall 2009; Cann and Wilhelm 2011; Hall 1995, 2001, 2007) finds that the candidates and voters in these elections behave similarly to their legislative and executive counterparts. In an interesting wrinkle, three states (Illinois, New Mexico, and Pennsylvania) initially select their judges in partisan elections, but these judges keep their positions in retention elections (more on these below).[1]

Nonpartisan Elections. Similarly, fifteen states utilize nonpartisan elections to select their judges. These are competitive elections, but the party identification of the candidates is not listed. Moreover, candidates have to survive a nonpartisan primary (often involving multiple candidates) in order to make it on the general election ballot. Michigan and Ohio have an interesting variation on this process as both allow political parties to nominate candidates. In Ohio, candidates run in a partisan primary, but then their partisan affiliation is removed on the general election ballot; in Michigan, candidates are nominated in partisan conventions.

Coding Michigan and Ohio is not straightforward. Most scholars code them as nonpartisan states since the party identification of the candidates is not on the ballot, thereby depriving voters of an important cue (Bonneau and Cann 2011; Bonneau and Hall 2009; Canes-Wrone, Clark, and Park 2012; Frederick and Streb 2008, 2011; Hall 2001; Hall and Bonneau 2006, 2008; Streb and Frederick 2009, 2011; Streb, Frederick, and LaFrance 2009). Other scholars code them as partisan states because political parties are more involved in the election process than they are in traditional nonpartisan states (e.g., Peters 2007, 2008, 2009; Streb, Frederick, and LaFrance 2007).[2] We prefer to categorize them as quasi-partisan in all our analyses: they are clearly more partisan than nonpartisan elections since political parties are involved in the nomination of candidates, but they are not as partisan as partisan elections due to the absence of the party cue on the ballot. This coding best describes both the formal ballot cues in those states and the actual nature of these elections. In chapter 3, however, for simplicity we treat them as nonpartisan (though replicating the results treating them as partisan has no substantively meaningful effect on the results).

Appointment. Twelve states use a form of appointment to staff their state high court benches. This appointment can either be by the governor or legislature (South Carolina and Virginia). In these states, judges are dependent on another branch of government for their selection and retention. While some states that utilize appointment also use a judicial nominating commission to constrain the choice made by the governor, the distinguishing feature of these systems is that the governor or legislature makes the appointment and that the judges never have to face the electorate to retain their positions.

Missouri Plan. The most popular method of selection in the states is the Missouri Plan, which is utilized by sixteen states. The method of selection is also called the "merit system." Here, a judicial nominating commission (the composition of which varies widely by state; see Fitzpatrick 2009) sends a list of three to five names to the governor. The governor is forced to select a nominee from this list. After a period of one to two years, the judge stands for retention in the next general election. The electorate is asked whether the judge should keep his or her job; if the judge receives a majority of "yes" votes, he or she serves a full term before facing the electorate again in another election. If the judge loses his or her bid for retention, the vacancy is filled using the same process described above.

There are several state-level variations in the process. First, as mentioned above, how the judicial nominating commission is selected and the mixture of lawyers and nonlawyers on it varies by state. Second, in some states the governor can reject the list of candidates from the nominating commission. If this happens, the commission must present the governor with a new slate of candidates. Third, some states require a judge to receive more than 50% of the vote to keep his or her job. In Illinois, judges must receive 60%; in New Mexico, 57%.

Despite all these variations, there are two key components necessary for a classification as a Missouri Plan state. First, the governor must be constrained in making an appointment by a judicial nominating commission. Second, judges must periodically face the electorate in a retention election (an election where multiple candidates are prohibited from running) in order to keep their positions.

Other variations. As if things were not complicated enough, there are five additional state-level variations in judicial selection worth mentioning.

First, two states (Michigan and West Virginia) elect their judges in multiseat elections.[3] Here, there are multiple candidates, and voters are able to vote for two. The top two vote-getters win the election. If there is an election for a partial term (due to retirement or death), that term is filled in a single-member election. Thus, you could have a situation where some elections in a year are single-member elections and others are multimember. This happened in Michigan in 2012.

Second, while most state supreme court elections are statewide, there are states that elect judges in districts. This occurs with all methods of selection: partisan (Illinois and Louisiana), nonpartisan (Kentucky and Mississippi), and retention (Maryland and Nebraska[4]). The nature of these districts varies: some have the same number of districts as justices; others have multiple justices representing a district. The general point is that these justices do not have to run for their office statewide; their geographical constituency is more limited.

Third, judicial elections are generally held at the same time as elections for other offices. However, a few states hold them at odd times (the spring) or in off years. And in other states, if a candidate wins a majority of the vote in the primary, this candidate is deemed the winner of the seat and does not appear on the general election ballot. Given the nature of the data we use in this book, we have to omit these states from our analysis since the Cooperative Congressional Election Study (CCES) was fielded at the time of the general election in 2010 and 2012. Fortunately, there are not a lot of states that do this (Arkansas, Georgia, Idaho, Oregon, Washington, and Wisconsin), but the dynamics of these elections tend to be different than elections held at the same time as normal elections. Of course, if no candidate receives 50% of the vote in the primary, then the top two vote-getters run in the general election, and they are included in our data.

Fourth, the size of the courts is not the same. In some states, there are only five justices; in others, there are seven or nine. In some states (such as Connecticut), judges decide cases in panels; in most, they decide cases en banc. Additionally, Texas and Oklahoma have two state supreme courts, one that deals with criminal cases and one that deals with civil cases.

Fifth, and finally, the term of office varies among the states. Only three states (Massachusetts, New Hampshire, and Rhode Island) have life tenure for its judges, though in New Jersey there is life tenure after one reappointment. In every other state—appointed and elected alike—judges have to be reappointed or reelected. The terms of office range from six to twelve years. This, coupled with the varying size of the courts, can make each election either more valuable (small court, long term: West Virginia) or less valuable (big court, short term: Texas).

The Changing Legal Landscape of Judicial Elections

Over the past decade, there have been several U.S. Supreme Court decisions that have changed the legal landscape governing the election of judges (Gaylord 2011). These changes have the potential to dramatically alter the nature and conduct of these elections. Here, we briefly summarize the central holdings and discuss how these decisions impact judicial elections. It is important to provide the legal and political context in which these elections operate because this has changed significantly over the past several years.

Republican Party of Minnesota v. White (536 US 765). In 2002, the U.S. Supreme Court struck down a provision in Minnesota's code of judicial ethics that prohibited candidates from announcing their views on legal and political issues (the "Announce Clause"). In a 5–4 decision, the Supreme Court held that such a prohibition violated the free speech rights of candidates. Essentially, if states choose to have judicial elections, they cannot "employ judicial elections while curbing the speech rights of candidates who run for judicial office" (Gaylord 2011, 1536). There were other provisions of the Minnesota code ("Pledges and Promises Clause," "Commit or Appear to Commit Clause," "Partisan Political Activity," "Solicitation Clause," and "Misrepresentation Rules") on which the Supreme Court declined to pass judgment (Hasen 2007). However, as one election law expert has said, while *White* did not decide these issues, "most of the important judicial campaign canons are subject to at least serious question under *White,* and the post-*White* trend in the lower courts has been discouraging for those who seek to defend the ABA code" (Hasen 2007, 30).

At the time *White* was decided, eight other states had similar provisions to the "Announce Clause" in their code of ethics (Caufield 2007; Hasen 2007). The concern was that this would lead to an explosion of campaign spending, candidates taking positions on issues that may come before the court, and a decline in legitimacy of the courts as candidates for the state high court bench began to campaign like other politicians (Caufield 2007; Margolies 2002; Schotland 2002).

Empirically, there has been little evidence that *White* has had a dramatic effect on judicial elections. Bonneau, Hall, and Streb (2011) examined elections before and after the *White* case at both the state supreme court and intermediate appellate court level. They found that, almost without exception, there was no measurable difference in elections pre- and post-*White* on such dimensions as campaign spending, electoral contestation, quality of candidates, and electoral competition. That being said, Bonneau, Hall, and Streb (2011) only look at simple bivariate relationships. Thus, we should be cautious about concluding too much from this study, though the results are suggestive.[5] Additionally, Michael J. Nelson (2011) finds that these "new-style" campaigns have not filtered down to the trial court level, and Arbour and McKenzie (2011, 18) conclude that "our results show that the fears of *White*'s critics appear overblown."

Caperton v. A.T. Massey Coal Co. (556 US 868). Another case involving judicial elections was handed down by the U.S. Supreme Court in 2009. In *Caperton,* the issue was recusal. Don Blankenship, the CEO of Massey Coal, spent over $3 million to help elect Justice Brent Benjamin to the West Virginia Supreme Court in 2004. In a 3–2 decision, Justice Benjamin voted with the majority to overturn a $50 million–verdict leveled against Massey Coal. Hugh Caperton appealed the decision to the U.S. Supreme Court, claiming that Justice Benjamin should be forced to recuse himself from the case because of the appearance of impropriety.

In a 5–4 decision, the U.S. Supreme Court ruled that, in this case, the appearance of impropriety was "extreme," and this appearance was enough to require recusal. Here, "the Court held that due process requires a judge to recuse herself when, based on 'objective and reasonable perceptions,' there is a 'probability of bias' by the judge towards one of the litigants" (Spektor and Zuckerman 2011, 987). Note that the court did not say there was actual impropriety; rather, they said that in certain cases, the "objective and reasonable perceptions" of bias are enough to require recusal. Of course, as Chief Justice Roberts pointed out in the dissent, the court did not take a position on such questions as how much money leads to this perception of bias or whether the holding is limited to campaign contributions in elections. What if a judicial candidate took a position on an issue during the election campaign that was contrary to the interests of a litigant (say, on tort reform)? Would this require recusal because of an appearance of bias? "Indeed, 'probability of bias' is as likely born out of a judicial candidate's speech against a litigant as it is out of a campaign contribution, as the *Caperton* dissent points out" (Spektor and Zuckerman 2011, 1004).

It is too soon to determine how *Caperton* will affect the conduct of judicial elections, especially given the tension between the holding there and the holding in *White* regarding candidates' speech. Some have argued that this uncertainty may be the least concerning aspect of *Caperton:* "the majority's decision, though, does more than simply create uncertainty; it also gives the public a reason to question the impartiality of the elected judiciary, which, in turn, does far more to undermine the state and federal judicial branches than the occasional extreme case like *Caperton*" (Gaylord 2011, 1541).[6]

Citizens United v. Federal Election Commission (558 US 310). Perhaps no recent U.S. Supreme Court decision has been more controversial than *Citizens United,* handed down in 2010. In this case, the Supreme Court struck down a provision of the Bipartisan Campaign Reform Act, which prohibited interest groups and unions from spending money to support (or oppose) a political candidate. In effect, these groups have the same free speech rights as individuals, and thus the government cannot infringe on these rights (Gaylord 2011). Just as individuals could spend as much money as they want on advertisements in support of a candidate, so can the Chamber of Commerce and the AFL-CIO. Obviously the details of the case (and the opinions of the justices) are far more complicated than this, but we are interested in the effects of this case for judicial elections and not in the detailed legal particularities of the case.

As for the effects on judicial elections, it is too soon to determine whether *Citizens United* has any significant or lasting impact. As has been reported, independent spending in judicial elections has been on the rise for the past decade or so (Skaggs et al. 2011). Thus, was the spending in 2012 simply a continuation of a trend that would have continued without the *Citizens United* case? At this point we simply do not know. However, if *Citizens United* has changed the landscape of elections in the United States (though it is far from clear this has happened), then we would expect it to affect judicial elections as well.

Arizona Free Enterprise Club's Freedom Club PAC v. Bennett (564 US ______). This case involves public financing and the use of rescue funds in the event one candidate opts for public financing and his or her opponent does not make the same choice and outspends the publicly financed candidate. North Carolina had such a system for their appellate court elections. If a candidate in the public financing program is outspent by a candidate outside the program, the publicly financed candidate is eligible for "rescue funds" to help eliminate the funding disparity: "the rescue money provisions are triggered in either the primary or the general election if more money is spent by a non-participant candidate or an independent group than the spending limit accepted by participating candidates" (Bend 2005, 600). This provision is crucial because without it, candidates might be reticent to opt-in to the public finance program out of concern they may be outspent dramatically by their opponents (Gaylord 2011).[7]

In 2011, the U.S. Supreme Court, in a 5–4 decision, struck down a "matching funds" provision in Arizona. The Supreme Court held that such rescue funds posed an unconstitutional burden on the free speech of privately financed candidates. In essence, by spending money to engage in political speech, candidates are penalized for their free speech because if they engage in speech, candidates know their opponents will be enabled by the government to do the same (Gaylord 2011). Thus, this is an unconstitutional burden on the free speech of privately financed political candidates. Indeed, in the 2004 North Carolina elections, no candidate or group spent enough money to trigger the rescue provisions, "and thus the provisions may have deterred non-participating candidates or independent groups from drastically outspending participating candidates" (Bend 2005, 602).

What does this mean for states with public financing, such as North Carolina? The ruling jeopardizes the success the program has had. According to North Carolina Voters for Clean Elections (2012), between 2004 and 2010, 77% of candidates for the North Carolina appellate courts participated in the program. Participants were winners and losers; Republicans and Democrats; incumbents and challengers; men and women; whites and nonwhites. In terms of the sources of campaign finance, prior to public finance, 73% of the funds raised by candidates came from attorneys, businesses, and so forth (excluding candidates' family funds); that fell to 14% after public financing. By these measures, the North Carolina program was a success. Given the concern the public has for the corrosive effects of campaign spending on the legitimacy of political institutions—courts as well as legislatures (Gibson 2012)—this decision invalidating the use of rescue funds could have far-reaching consequences on the North Carolina program.

In sum, these four Supreme Court rulings issued over the past twelve years have the potential to transform the nature of Supreme Court elections. While we do not have longitudinal data in this book, we are able to situate our findings in the literature to ascertain whether the nature of these races is the same as in the past. Moreover, for the first time, we bring individual-level data to bear on fundamental issues of voter participation and vote choice in these elections. The result is the most comprehensive treatment to date of voter behavior in state supreme court elections.

Judicial Elections in the 2000s

The changes in electoral competition and campaign spending that state supreme court elections witnessed in the 1990s (Bonneau and Hall 2009) have reached new levels in the past decade (Skaggs et al. 2011), though Kritzer (2011) demonstrates that electoral competition really has not significantly changed outside the South. While these elections continue to be hotly contested (especially in states with partisan elections), the amount of interest group participation and campaign spending has reached a whole new level. Indeed, some critics of judicial elections (e.g., Brandenburg and Caufield 2009) have argued that the existing evidence on them (e.g., Bonneau and Hall 2009; Hall and Bonneau 2006, 2008) is out-of date because the nature of these elections has fundamentally changed since the end of their data (either 2000 or 2004, depending on the analysis). We just discussed the changing legal environment of these elections; here, we discuss some changes to the conduct of judicial elections over the past decade.

Perhaps the biggest change has been the amount of campaign spending in these elections and the more widespread participation of interest groups and political action committees (PACs) (Skaggs et al. 2011). While this is certainly noteworthy, it is unclear what the effects of these changes are; that is, it is unclear whether these groups have more influence now than they did, say, ten years ago. This is particularly true since scholars have found that campaign spending has diminishing marginal returns (Bonneau 2007b; Bonneau and Cann 2011). These changes could have two potential impacts. First, they could contribute to the appearance that a justice is for sale and contribute to the erosion of legitimacy for the judiciary. However, in the most comprehensive study of this to date, Gibson (2012; Gibson et al. 2011) demonstrates that judicial elections actually contribute to judicial legitimacy, not erode it. Second, if scholars like Bonneau and Hall (2009) are correct, then this increase in spending provides the voters with more information about the candidates and the election, and thus will increase both participation and meaningful participation. While we do not address the first potential consequence here, we are able to say something about the second: has voter participation (and meaningful participation) changed over the past decade?

The other big change (though it is too soon to tell if this is just an aberration or indicative of something more systematic) over the past few years has been in the conduct of retention elections. In 2010, three justices in Iowa lost their bids for retention for the first time in the history of the state. The key issue in the race was their vote on a case legalizing same-sex marriage. Additionally, the justices decided not to campaign to retain their positions, arguing that they should be judged on criteria such as competence and not based on their substantive rulings (Sulzberger 2010). In addition to these three judges, there were opposition campaigns against state supreme court judges in a few other states (Aspin 2011): Alaska (Fabe), Colorado (Bender, Martinez, and Rice), Florida (Labarga and Perry), Kansas (Beier, Biles, Nuss, and Luckert), and Illinois (Kilbride). All of these justices were retained, leading Aspin (2011, 232) to conclude "there is little evidence to support a prediction that they . . . mark the beginning of a substantial increase in the removal of judges for political reasons."

This can be seen by a quick look at the 2012 elections. Justices in Iowa and Florida were once again targeted by opposition groups upset with the content of some of the justices' rulings. However, these justices easily kept their seats. Part of this was the decision made by the justices to make public appearances and take seriously the threat of losing their jobs. That being said, the increase in challenges to incumbent judges in retention elections has been higher in recent years. While judges have been challenged in the past (and lost), such challenges appear to be becoming more widespread over the past two election cycles, though again we cannot tell at this point if this represents a sea change in the conduct of these elections. Here, we offer the most systematic examination of state supreme court retention elections to date, looking at the determinants of participation and vote choice across races as well as across states.

Plan for This Book

We set out to answer fundamental questions about the nature of contemporary state supreme court elections and the behavior of voters. Unlike past studies that rely heavily (or exclusively) on aggregate-level data, we have individual-level data on voter participation in vote choice on state supreme court elections in 2010 and 2012. We compliment this data with race- and candidate-specific factors to present a comprehensive treatment of voter behavior. Finally, we use experiments to ascertain the effects of specific institutional variations in these elections (partisanship, occupational cues, incumbency) and, for the first time, are able to determine the precise effects of these variations on electoral behavior and outcomes.

Chapter 1 focuses on the factors that determine whether or not a voter participates in an election to the state high court bench. We hypothesize that a variety of state institutional characteristics, individual-level characteristics, and campaign characteristics influence the decision to participate in judicial elections. We focus chiefly here on the partisan nature of the ballot and expect that when the candidates' partisan identification is provided on the ballot, voters are more likely to participate in the election.

While campaign-level factors have been studied at the aggregate level, we bring information from the 2010 and 2012 CCES surveys to shed light on the effects of individual voter characteristics and, where appropriate, the interaction between voter characteristics and campaign-related factors. Drawing on the literature on voter participation for presidential and congressional elections (e.g., Brady, Verba, and Schlozman 1995; Caldeira, Patterson, and Markko 1985; J. Campbell 1987; Hillygus 2005; Rosenstone and Hanson 1993), we utilize the 2010 and 2012 CCES surveys to assess voter participation. Using two years of surveys also allows us to compare changes between a presidential election year (2012) and a midterm election (2010).

In chapter 2, we turn our focus to the vote choice of respondents, explicating the factors that lead an individual to vote for one candidate over another. Although we discuss several factors that could determine vote choice, we again focus primarily on the role of partisanship. Partisanship is a critically important heuristic for voters because it provides simple meaningful cues for complex political decisions (Kam 2005) and is relevant to a wide range of political choices (Huckfeldt et al. 1999).

While it is difficult to overstate the importance of party identification in the political behavior literature, there is a large set of elections to which the applicability of partisanship is questionable: those that are nominally nonpartisan. While elections for national office and many state offices are traditional partisan elections, about three-fourths of municipal elections are nonpartisan (DeSantis and Renner 1991), as are those for many judges, school board officers, and even the Nebraska state legislature.

Using the 2010 and 2012 CCES data allows us to explore the extent to which nonpartisan elections effectively screen out the partisanship of candidates. If nonpartisan elections are effective, then voters' partisan affiliation should be unrelated to their decision to vote for the candidate who is their co-partisan. However, if candidates are effectively able to signal their partisan affiliation to voters in nonpartisan elections, then voters should vote for their co-partisans in equal proportions in both partisan and nonpartisan elections.

While the 2010 and 2012 CCES data are the first national individual-level data on voters' choices in judicial elections, observational data can take us only so far. The data allow us to ascertain whether there is a relationship or not, but they do not allow us to ascertain *why* such a relationship occurs. For that, we need to conduct some controlled experiments.

In chapter 3, we conduct a series of experiments in which we provide subjects with characteristics of candidates running for the state supreme court. We use actual campaign ads run by candidates to make the vignettes as realistic as possible. However, in addition to simply varying whether we provide the partisan affiliation of the candidate, we also vary the intensity of the information we present to voters.

Our goal is simply to determine whether providing subjects in a carefully controlled lab experiment with candidates' issue positions and background allows subjects to correctly ascertain the party identification of the candidates. If this information is consistent with our large-N analysis in chapter 2, then we will have persuasive evidence that nonpartisan elections are effective (or ineffective) at shielding the partisan affiliation of candidates from the voters.

In chapter 4, we examine the role of incumbency. In another institutional feature unique to judicial elections, some states denote which candidate is the incumbent on the ballot. Thus, voters are reminded, before casting their votes, which candidate is the current officeholder. Additionally, the governor in most states appoints an interim replacement to fill vacancies on the bench. This is not a rare event: roughly one-third of incumbents initially attain their positions this way. Consequently, some incumbents have previously won election to the bench, while other incumbents have never won a competitive election. We would expect these different types of incumbents would not be similarly advantaged. In this chapter, we conduct an experiment randomly assigning subjects to groups to examine (1) the effects of denoting incumbency on the ballot and (2) the differences between elected incumbents and appointed incumbents. We also condition the treatment based on whether the election is a partisan election or nonpartisan election. This treatment of incumbency goes far beyond how scholars commonly analyze it, and the institutional variation that exists in state supreme court elections provides an ideal environment to test theories of incumbency.

A plurality of states select their judges using the "merit selection" system, where judges are appointed to a short initial term before they are placed on the ballot for a retention election. Retention elections afford voters an opportunity to weigh in on whether a judge should be kept in office. However, we understand very little about how citizens decide how to vote in these elections. Even more so than other judicial elections, retention elections are very low-information affairs. Candidates only rarely put up campaign signs, distribute materials, run ads, or spend any money at all on their retention elections. As such, what information do voters have to go on in such a low-information environment?

In chapter 5, we evaluate factors that motivate participation in retention elections. We then create a framework for explaining citizen choice in these elections. We hypothesize that citizens may still be influenced by their partisanship and the retention candidate's party identification. Moreover, we evaluate whether the retention candidate's tenure and status as chief versus associate judge influence voters' willingness to support the judge in a retention election. We assess whether anti-retention campaigns affect voters' general predisposition to simply vote "yes" in retention elections, and, finally, we test for race and gender biases in citizens' expressed vote choices in retention elections. The 2012 CCES includes the voting decisions of voters in retention elections and provides the individual-level data we need to better understand voting in retention elections.

Our conclusion summarizes and unifies our major empirical results. We discuss current conversations about reforming the method of judicial selection that are happening in several state legislatures and use our results to make predictions about how the conduct of judicial elections will change in these states if they adopt certain institutional reforms under discussion.

We also discuss the changing nature of the normative debate surrounding judicial elections. While this debate used to be characterized by a debate over independence versus accountability, it has now shifted to one of more transparency versus less transparency. Scholars agree that all judges are both independent and accountable, though some systems promote one concept over the other, and judges are certainly independent from and accountable to different political actors depending on the method of selection. Acknowledging that politics enters the selection process even in the federal judiciary (where judges are appointed for life), the debate has begun to shift to which systems promote the most transparency versus those that attempt to keep the politics behind closed doors. Indeed, even the most "secretive" method of selection (the Missouri Plan) is facing (and responding to) calls to be more open and transparent in the decision-making process.

Finally, we discuss the implications of our results for (1) lower court elections and (2) elections for other down-ballot offices. We also discuss future issues that are likely to emerge in judicial elections.

1

INDIVIDUAL-LEVEL FACTORS AND VOTER PARTICIPATION IN STATE SUPREME COURT ELECTIONS

When you go into the ballot box and see a whole list of judges' names on a ballot, and you don't know anything about them, it's a hopeless mess. People just, in many cases, don't vote at all.
—Sandra Day O'Connor, "Keynote Address by Justice Sandra Day O'Connor"

The conventional wisdom about the nature of judicial elections, espoused by interest groups, the media, and policymakers, includes two claims: first, voters do not know anything about judicial elections or the candidates running in them; second, in many cases voters opt not to vote at all. We address the first point in chapters 2 and 3. In this chapter, we address the second claim and investigate the determinants of voter participation in state supreme court elections focusing on the impact of institutional arrangements.

For decades, scholars of politics have been interested in the determinants of political participation. In order for elections to fulfill their purpose as effective mechanisms by which citizens can participate in the functioning of government, it is imperative that we understand the factors that make citizens more (or less) likely to participate in the political process. Scholars have spilled copious amounts of ink examining the causes of political participation, largely focusing on federal elections (Freedman, Franz, and Goldstein 2004; Henderson and Chatfield 2011; Kam and Palmer 2008;

Krasno and Green 2008; Riker and Ordeshook 1968; Rosenstone and Hansen 1993; Sondheimer and Green 2010; Wolfinger and Rosenstone 1980). Only recently have political scientists turned their attention to down-ballot elections (but see Dubois 1979; Bonneau and Hall 2009; Bullock and Dunn 1996; Hall 2007; Schaffner, Streb, and Wright 2001).

In this chapter, we seek to answer a simple yet unanswered question: what factors influence an individual's decision to participate in a state supreme court election? More specifically, we are interested in the differences between partisan elections and nonpartisan elections. Do partisan elections increase voter participation compared to nonpartisan elections? At least since the time of the Progressives over a hundred years ago, partisan elections have been frequently criticized for depressing the number of candidates, thereby stifling competition, and for making election officials beholden to their own political party at the expense of their constituents (Duncan 1913; Gould 1986; Hofstadter 1955). Regardless of the empirical validity of these charges, the costs of partisan elections may be outweighed by their benefits. Here, we examine one such potential benefit: increased voter participation.

In order to examine the effects of the partisan ballot on voter participation, we first need an office where occupants are selected by both partisan and nonpartisan elections. Fortunately, state supreme courts provide exactly such an environment, allowing us to isolate the effect of ballot type while holding the office constant. Indeed, state supreme courts have three forms of elections by which judges are selected: competitive partisan elections (partisan affiliation of candidates on the ballot), competitive nonpartisan elections (no partisan affiliation of candidates on the ballot), and noncompetitive retention elections (where judges are simply subjected to a yes/no vote on whether they should remain in office). In this chapter, we limit our analysis to the comparison between partisan, quasi-partisan, and nonpartisan elections. We examine retention elections in chapter 6.

The second thing we need is individual-level data on voter participation across different states. Without this, we cannot ascertain the determinants of the behavior of individual voters. While existing studies of voter participation in state supreme court elections have gone a long way toward explaining the variance in voter participation rates (Bonneau and Hall 2009; Dubois 1979; Hall 2007), these studies all utilize aggregate-level data (but see Johnson, Schaefer, and McKnight 1978). Thus, these studies cannot tell us anything about the individual-level variables determining participation in judicial elections. We use the 2010 and 2012 nationwide CCES surveys in order to alleviate this limitation.

Our results indicate that the factors that predict general turnout differ to some extent from those that determine participation in judicial elections. We show that state institutional factors, particularly the partisan format of the election, as well as individual factors such as education, gender, and union membership are strong predictors of participation in judicial elections. In sum, consistent with prior work and contrary to some claims, voter participation in state supreme court elections is affected by voter characteristics, the context of the election, and the rules under which the election occurs.

Partisanship and Voter Participation

The debate over the effects of partisanship on voter participation dates back to the early twentieth century. As mentioned above, the Progressives embarked on a campaign to purge partisanship from elections. As it relates to voter participation, the Progressives argued that "an active and properly motivated citizenry does not need party labels" (Schaffner, Streb, and Wright 2001, 8). The electorate should simply choose the candidates that are best qualified to run the government effectively and efficiently; party labels are unrelated to these characteristics. Thus, elections should be nonpartisan.

However, removing partisan affiliation from the ballot deprives voters of a key piece of meaningful information. It has been well established in the political science literature that one of the best cues for voters to determine which candidates best reflect their ideology and policy positions is the partisan affiliation of the candidate (e.g., Aldrich 1995; Page and Shapiro 1992). That is, if a voter is a Democrat, then any Democratic candidate for an office will better represent the voter's policy positions than any Republican candidate for an office. As Schaffner, Streb, and Wright (2001, 9) say, "It follows, then, that taking party labels away in nonpartisan elections and thereby raising the costs of information about candidates for voters, nonpartisan elections would make voting more difficult and thereby undermine the potential for popular control." Due to the removal of an important piece of information from the ballot, voters may lack enough information to feel sufficiently informed to cast a vote. When voters feel uninformed, participation will decrease (Downs 1957; Hall 2007).

Schaffner, Streb, and Wright (2001) find evidence consistent with this. They find lower levels of voter participation when a nonpartisan ballot is used compared to a partisan ballot (see tables 4 and 6). In judicial elections, Dubois (1979) was the first to find that there was higher participation in partisan elections compared to nonpartisan elections. More recently, Hall (2007) and Bonneau and Hall (2009) document that, on average, there are higher amounts of ballot roll-off (lower amounts of voter participation) in states that utilize nonpartisan elections versus partisan elections. In addition to the aggregate data, Bonneau and Hall (2009) examine two states that recently switched from partisan elections to nonpartisan elections (Arkansas and North Carolina). They find that voter participation decreased significantly in both states after the move to nonpartisan elections. As further evidence of the effects of switching away from partisan elections, Dubois (1979, 875) examined four states that switched from partisan elections to retention elections in the 1948–74 period, and the results "demonstrate the dramatic depressing effect upon turnout when voters are deprived simultaneously of meaningful voting cues and an electoral choice." Thus, there are good theoretical and empirical reasons to suspect that nonpartisan elections serve to decrease voter participation.

Participation and Judicial Elections

The advantage of examining voter participation in judicial elections is that these elections provide three different types of election in which we can examine voter participation. This source of institutional variation forms the basis for our primary hypotheses.

In some states, judges are selected in partisan elections. These are equivalent to the traditional type of election for most major offices in the United States: each major political party (Democratic and Republican) has a candidate on the ballot, and the partisan affiliations of each are noted on the ballot so voters know, at the time they cast their votes, which candidate represents which party. We hypothesize that voter participation will be highest under this institutional setup. There are two reasons for this. First, as discussed above, this provides voters with an important piece of information that will help guide their vote choice. When voters feel more informed, they participate in higher numbers (Bonneau and Hall 2009; Downs 1957; Hall 2007). Second, and relatedly, voters who vote a straight party ticket will also have their vote registered for judicial candidates as well. Thus, all voters who select the straight party option have their vote recorded for every representative of that party on the ballot; there is no possibility for voters to skip an office. Consequently, even if the voters had no information about the candidates, if they were to vote a straight ticket, their vote would be recorded for all offices (Bonneau and Loepp 2014).

Another method of judicial selection is nonpartisan elections. In these states, multiple candidates run in contested elections; however, the partisan identification of the candidates is not provided on the ballot to the voters. Indeed, it is possible for both candidates to be from one political party in these states. This lack of information leads us to expect that voters will be less likely to participate in these elections compared to partisan elections. Additionally, voters who utilize the straight party ticket option would not have their votes counted for the judicial races, since these races are nonpartisan. Individuals who vote a straight ticket would need to vote for judicial races separately; voters might not be aware of this and thus might accidentally fail to participate in the election even when they intended to do so (Bonneau and Loepp 2014).

Two states, Ohio and Michigan, use a quasi-partisan hybrid of the partisan and nonpartisan systems. In this system, parties are allowed to nominate and endorse candidates as in a partisan system. However, the ballot itself is nonpartisan because candidates' party affiliations are not shown alongside the candidates' names (as they are in other partisan elections). We expect voter participation in these races to be higher than it is in traditional nonpartisan elections (since there is party involvement) but lower than in traditional partisan elections (since the partisan affiliation of candidates is not on the general election ballot, and Michigan has the straight-ticket voting option, meaning that voters who utilize this will not have their votes recorded for the state supreme court races).[1]

Finally, some states utilize retention elections to keep judges on the bench. These elections are structured more like referenda than they are competitive elections, though unlike referenda incumbents in retention elections nearly always win. Unlike partisan and nonpartisan elections, retention elections do not provide the voters with a choice between candidates. Rather, voters are simply asked whether Judge X should keep his or her job. If a majority of them agree,[2] then the judge keeps his or her position for another fixed term of office (six to twelve years). Retention races are characterized by a lack of campaigning and high affirmative vote totals for the incumbent (Bonneau and Hall 2009). As such, we omit retention elections from this chapter, leaving participation in retention elections for chapter 5.

The presence or absence of partisan labels in judicial elections is, at its core, an informational problem. From among the host of individual-level variables that predict voter turnout generally, the individual voter characteristics that we expect will have the greatest impact on turnout will be those that are related to voters' levels of information. For example, we would expect education to influence participation in judicial elections more than home ownership because education has more direct bearing on a person's level of information than home ownership.

In sum, we hypothesize:

H1.1: A voter is more likely to participate when he or she is provided with the partisan affiliations of the candidates.

H1.2: Individual-level factors related to the level of information of citizens will have larger effects than individual-level factors that are simply demographic in nature.

Data

To better understand the dynamics of voter participation in judicial elections, we utilize data from the 2012 and 2010 Cooperative Congressional Election Study (CCES). The CCES is a national stratified matched sample of voters that is administered through a web-based platform on computers or other web-enabled devices. Cross-validation of the CCES against mail and random-digit dial telephone methods suggests that the CCES provides a nationally representative sample (Ansolabehere and Schaffner 2011). The CCES is segmented into modules of a thousand respondents each, with the first half of the survey composed of common content asked of respondents on all modules. The second half of the survey is devoted to team content created by the respective sponsoring institutions. More information about the CCES can be found in appendix A.

On the 2010 CCES, judicial vote choice questions were asked on three modules of one thousand respondents each. Because we can only use responses from states where there were contested judicial elections, our sample size using the 2010 data is just over $n = 1000$. The 2012 CCES featured judicial vote choice on the common content, giving us thousands of respondents who lived in states holding contested judicial elections. In 2012, all CCES respondents living in a state holding a contested judicial election were asked about their participation in one randomly assigned state supreme court race in their state. A list of the races analyzed in this chapter can be found in appendix B.

Rather than examining voter turnout in judicial elections, because few, if any, voters come to the polls simply to participate in a judicial election, it is more appropriate to look at the extent to which voters who have already come to the polls to participate in up-ballot races decide to cast a vote in a judicial election. The failure to vote in a down-ballot race after voting for higher offices is known as ballot roll-off. For example, if one hundred people turn out to vote for president and ninety of these people vote in the state supreme court race, ballot roll-off is 10%. Higher levels of ballot roll-off reflect lower levels of voter participation.

We can take an initial look at the data as a simple test of H1.1 by simply showing the proportion of individuals in each election format who voted in a race for higher office (using verified turnout),[3] but who did not report voting in a judicial race. For this initial examination, we rely on only the 2012 CCES due to its larger sample size (the sample includes 7,265 individuals who voted for higher offices who could have also chosen to vote in a contested state supreme court election). Figure 1.1 shows the proportion of ballot roll-off by election format (nonpartisan, quasi-partisan, and partisan).

Consistent with the findings of previous studies, our survey results suggest that nonpartisan elections have the highest rates of ballot roll-off of the three election formats we consider, with nearly one-fifth of voters opting to not participate in a judicial election in spite of voting for higher offices. In quasi-partisan elections roll-off is reduced to about 13% of voters, while partisan elections in 2012 exhibited roll-off of less than 10%. The differences in roll-off across election formats are statistically significant as evidenced by the lack of overlap of the 95% confidence intervals. The evidence from the 2012 CCES is strongly supportive of the hypothesis that nonpartisan elections depress participation.

A Two-Stage Model of Participation in Judicial Elections

While this evidence is striking, a more sophisticated analysis is necessary to test hypotheses about individual-level variables that may influence turnout. Moreover, it is necessary to control for additional factors that may be correlated with both roll-off and election format in order to get unbiased estimates of the effects of election format on roll-off. Finally, due to fact that we only observe roll-off for individuals who have voted, there is a possibility of selection

FIGURE 1.1. Rates of ballot roll-off by election format, 2012 CCES

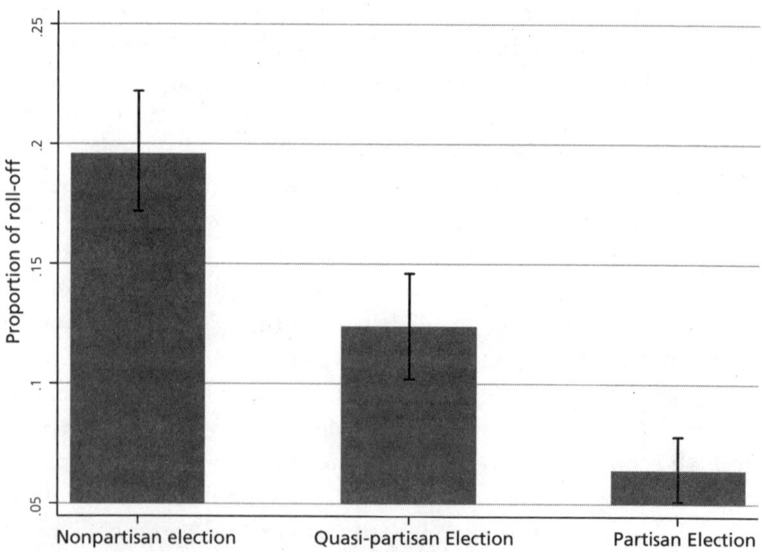

Note: Data from the 2012 CCES with $n = 7{,}265$. Capped range bars represent 95% confidence intervals.

bias if the error terms across the turnout and roll-off equations are correlated. As such, we proceed in the next section to develop a more sophisticated statistical model of voter turnout and ballot roll-off.

As we move to build such a model, our dependent variable of primary interest remains ballot roll-off. Recognizing that few (if any) voters are driven to the polls solely out of interest in a judicial race, though, we conceptualize participation in judicial elections as a two-stage process where initially citizens choose to vote an up-ballot race for president, governor, U.S. House, and/or U.S. Senate (*Turnout*) and then choose whether to participate in a particular judicial election (*Roll-off*). For the turnout variable, we use the validated measure of electoral participation rather than the self-reported measure (Ansolabehere and Hersh 2012).[4] We can then build a two-stage model to account for turnout generally and roll-off (nonparticipation in a down-ballot race) specifically. The model predicts these two dependent variables using separate but overlapping sets of independent variables.

VARIABLES PREDICTING TURNOUT

In the first-stage equation of our model, we delineate the factors that predict a voters' decision to come to the polls at all (*Turnout*). In the phase in which a voter is deciding to participate in an election, we suspect that factors specific to a judicial election have minimal impact (Bonneau and Hall 2009; Hall and Bonneau 2008). Simply put, voters do not show up at the polls to participate in only judicial elections. Instead, the factors that determine turnout are driven by the characteristics of individual voters and the characteristics of up-ballot races in the voter's state.

In terms of voter characteristics, education (*Education*) stands out among demographic factors as a particularly important predictor of turnout. More educated citizens are more likely to vote than those with less education, likely due to the fact that education lowers informational costs associated with voting (Brady, Verba, and Schlozman 1995; Timpone 1998; Wolfinger and Rosenstone 1980). We measure education by whether or not the individual has earned a college degree, and we expect that more educated individuals are more likely to turn out.

Historically, African Americans and other minorities have faced unique impediments to registration and voting; studies have shown that Caucasian voters (*White*) continue to have higher rates of participation than minorities, even controlling for other factors (Caldeira, Patterson, and Markko 1985; Shaw, de la Garza, and Lee 2000). Consistent with this, we hypothesize that white individuals are more likely to vote than nonwhite individuals.

We also include a dichotomous indicator for gender, as some studies have shown that gender has a modest effect on turnout, with men (*Male*) typically voting at lower rates than women (Carroll and Fox 2009; Timpone 1998). We expect that result to hold here as well.

Connections with various community groups that often offer reminders of participation have been shown to increase voting. We include variables for respondents who are either union members or live in a household with a union member (*Union*) (Leighley and Nagler 2007) or who attend church at least weekly (*Weekly church attendance*) (Timpone 1998). Union households and individuals who attend church are more likely to vote than individuals who are not from union households or who do not attend church at least weekly.

Along the lines of community connectedness, homeowners (*Homeowner*) are more likely to feel a stake in their community, to have an interest in the long-term future of their community and state, and to believe they will be in a location long enough to make it worthwhile to register and determine the appropriate voting location. These types of characteristics make homeowners more likely to vote (DiPasquale and Glaeser 1999).

In addition to voter characteristics, the nature of politics in a citizen's state may affect their probability of turning out. States with competitive elections have higher levels of turnout (Cann and Cole 2011; Cox and Munger 1989). We operationalize the competitiveness of a state's political environment (*Competitive environment*) using Ceasar and Saldin's (2005) Major Party Index (MPI), which is a weighted average of the outcomes of presidential, congressional, gubernatorial, and state legislative elections and ranges from 100 (perfectly Republican) to 0 (perfectly Democratic). To transform the MPI to a measure of competitiveness, we take the absolute deviation of the MPI from 50. We use MPI values from the 2008 election, the election cycle immediately prior to the collection of the 2010 data.[5] The more competitive the state electoral environment, the more likely an individual is to vote.

Beyond the general competitiveness of a state, a close race for major office can boost turnout. As such, we include dichotomous indicators for a close gubernatorial race (*Close gubernatorial race*) in a state and a close U.S. Senate race (*Close senate race*) in a state. Races are designated as "close" if they were categorized by RealClearPolitics.com as a "toss-up" race just prior to the election. Individuals in states with close races for Senate or governor are more likely to turn out.

VARIABLES PREDICTING STATE SUPREME COURT ELECTION BALLOT ROLL-OFF

Once a voter has decided to participate in the higher-profile races that draw voters to the polls, voters must decide whether to vote in a state supreme court election. If they do not, they are said to roll-off. As ballot roll-off increases, voter participation decreases. To some extent, we expect the factors that affect turnout to affect roll-off as well. In the same way that education reduces the information costs of voting generally, it may decrease roll-off in judicial elections by reducing information costs in judicial elections specifically. In studies using aggregate data on judicial elections, Hall (2007) finds that states with more educated populations have lower aggregate roll-off, but Streb, Frederick, and LaFrance (2009) find no significant effect. Importantly, Nichols and Strizek (1995) contend that the effect of education on turnout is often masked in aggregate data; our use of individual-level data allows us to address this question head-on for the first time with a national sample.

For our variables associated with group membership and community connectedness, we expect that the same factors promoting voting (information coming from a union or church and the stronger ties to community that come with home ownership) will also decrease roll-off in judicial elections. For purely demographic traits such as race and gender, it is unclear whether the same things that drive women and whites to the polls in larger numbers will lead them to complete the ballot at higher rates than men and minorities. Indeed, we see it as possible that if men and minorities overcome the respective reasons that their demographics turn out in lower numbers, they may be more likely to complete the ballot than women and whites.

While factors influencing electoral competitiveness generally in the state (such as competitive gubernatorial and Senate races and the MPI-based state competitiveness measure) may boost participation in up-ballot races, we see no theoretical reason that such factors would affect rates of roll-off in judicial elections. Hence, we omit these variables from the second stage of the model.

Beyond the factors that influence turnout, there are a number of factors unique to judicial elections that may influence roll-off in these elections. The foremost among these is the presence of partisan cues in the election (*Partisan*). Evidence at the aggregate level suggests that partisan cues in elections give voters a simple means by which to distinguish between two candidates that they would otherwise know nothing about (e.g., Bonneau and Hall 2009). The presence of a partisan cue gives voters enough specific information about the candidates to make them feel as though they can make an informed decision. As such we expect partisan election states to have higher voter participation than nonpartisan states. Ohio and Michigan use a quasi-partisan system for electing judges where parties nominate judges, and the party affiliation of judges often circulates during the campaigns, but party affiliations are not actually listed on the ballot (as they are in partisan elections). As such, we expect roll-off to be higher in quasi-partisan election states (*Quasi-partisan*) than in partisan states but lower than in nonpartisan states (nonpartisan serves as the reference category against which voters in partisan and quasi-partisan states are compared).

Another factor that provides voting cues to citizens is incumbency. If voters know a particular candidate is an incumbent (*Incumbent*), they can use their opinion of their state's justice system to inform their decision (a favorable view of their state's justice system would imply a vote for the incumbent; an unfavorable view would lead them toward voting against the incumbent). As incumbents often enjoy better name recognition than challengers, and as some states even formally identify the incumbent on the ballot, more voters may feel they have more information about the race when the race involves an incumbent, leading to lower roll-off rates.[6]

Finally, the nature of the campaign in the judicial election may lower roll-off rates. Recognizing that these effects may be difficult to pick up at the individual level (particularly since there are only twenty races involved in the November 2012 election and another eighteen in the November 2010 election from which our data are drawn), which limits our observed variation at the campaign level, we nevertheless include them to control for any effects they may have. Specifically, we look at the combined per capita spending (*Per capita spending*) of the candidates in a judicial election and whether or not there is a quality challenger (a candidate who has held a previous judicial position) in a race (*Quality challenger*). Aggregate analyses of a large number of races over many years suggests that races with more spending and those that are competitive because of the presence of a quality challenger have higher participation (Bonneau and Hall 2009; Hall and Bonneau 2006).

Results

Because of the two-stage nature of the choice we are modeling (first to turn out to vote at all and second whether to roll-off on a judicial election), we analyze our data using a probit model with Heckman's sample selection correction (Van de Ven and Van Pragg 1981). If the errors in the two equations are correlated, the estimates of the parameters in the roll-off equation would be biased in a single-equation probit model. As the degree of that correlation is an open question, it is appropriate to proceed without making the assumption of uncorrelated errors.

The results of the model appear in table 1.1. Before analyzing our primary question, participation in the judicial election, we quickly review the first-stage equation of general turnout. The turnout equation has few surprises, with college-educated citizens, regular church attendees, and homeowners being more likely to turn out in both 2010 and 2012. The presence of contested up-ballot races exerts influence as well, through gubernatorial races in 2012 and Senate races in 2010 (though turnout was modestly lower in states with close Senate races in 2012). Higher MPI deviations from 50% were associated with slightly higher turnout in 2010, while we observed the opposite effect in 2012; still, neither of those effects is large enough to be substantively meaningful. In our 2010 data, men were slightly more

TABLE 1.1 Heckman probit model of general turnout and state supreme court election roll-off, 2012 and 2010 CCES

	2012		2010	
	ROLL-OFF	TURNOUT	ROLL-OFF	TURNOUT
Partisan	−0.177* (0.060)	—	−0.510* (0.227)	—
Quasi-partisan	−0.184* (0.040)	—	−0.449* (0.243)	—
Incumbent	0.119* (0.049)	—	−0.097 (0.135)	—
Quality challenger	−0.071 (0.045)	—	−0.245 (0.183)	—
Per capita spending	0.056 (0.041)	—	2.104* (1.013)	—
College-educated	−0.371* (0.049)	0.393* (0.099)	0.319 (0.221)	0.373* (0.124)
White	−0.072 (0.063)	0.099 (0.066)	0.073 (0.206)	0.152 (0.154)
Male	−0.012 (0.046)	0.016 (0.050)	−0.354 (0.191)	0.372* (0.130)
Weekly church attendance	−0.182* (0.051)	0.228* (0.056)	−0.113 (0.248)	0.512* (0.140)
Union member in household	−0.072 (0.068)	0.073 (0.078)	0.700* (0.257)	−0.094 (0.208)
Homeowner	−0.379* (0.051)	0.399* (0.054)	−0.245 (0.253)	0.303* (0.150)
Competitive environment	—	−0.020* (0.008)	—	0.076* (0.027)
Close senate race	—	−0.243* (0.106)	—	0.907* (0.271)
Close gubernatorial Race	—	0.268* (0.037)	—	−0.042 (0.187)
Constant	0.083 (0.076)	0.209* (0.088)	−0.786 (0.970)	−0.941* (0.269)
Wald χ^2	152.95* ($p < 0.001$)		43.05* ($p < 0.001$)	
ρ	−0.997 (0.005)		0.009 (0.807)	
Wald test of $\rho = 0$	11.48 ($p < 0.001$)		0.0001 ($p = 0.991$)	
n	9,086 (7,265 uncensored/ 1821 censored)		1,045 (772 uncensored/ 273 censored)	

Note: *$p < 0.05$, two-tailed. Standard errors in parentheses

likely to turnout than women, but we observe no such gender effect in the larger 2012 sample. Race and union membership exerted no significant effect on turnout in either 2010 or 2012.

Looking at the equation of primary interest, the second-stage estimates of factors affecting roll-off in state supreme court elections, there are a number of interesting findings. First and foremost, the importance of partisan cues should not be understated. Voters in partisan election states are significantly less likely to roll-off than those in nonpartisan election states. The same is true of voters in quasi-partisan states. In the 2012 election the difference in roll-off rates between partisan and quasi-partisan elections was not statistically significant; in 2010 roll-off rates were modestly lower among respondents voting in partisan elections than those voting in quasi-partisan elections.

To offer a more readily interpretable expression of the effects of the coefficients in the model, we present a table of predicted probabilities in table 1.2. The numbers in the table reflect the probability of roll-off conditional on a citizen having turned out and are computed based on the mean (for continuous variables) or modal (for categorical variables) values of the variables in the model, except for

TABLE 1.2 Predicted probabilities of roll-off, 2012 CCES

VARIABLE	VARIED VALUES	PREDICTED PROBABILITY (STANDARD ERROR)	95% CONFIDENCE INTERVAL
Election Format	Partisan	0.043 (0.012)	(0.006, 0.080)
	Quasi-partisan	0.040 (0.017)	(0.008, 0.073)
	Nonpartisan	0.131 (0.024)	(0.085, 0.177)
Incumbency	Incumbent	0.131 (0.024)	(0.085, 0.177)
	Non-incumbent	0.070 (0.029)	(0.013, 0.127)
College	College degree	0.096 (0.017)	(0.062, 0.130)
	No college degree	0.131 (0.024)	(0.085, 0.177)
Church attendance	Weekly church	0.125 (0.023)	(0.080, 0.170)
	Not weekly	0.131 (0.024)	(0.085, 0.177)
Homeownership	Homeowner	0.131 (0.024)	(0.085, 0.177)
	Not homeowner	0.168 (0.036)	(0.098, 0.238)

Note: Predicted probabilities are calculated based on the 2012 results presented in table 1.1.

the noted characteristic being varied. Given the much larger sample size in the 2012 CCES data, we calculate the predicted probabilities for those data.[7] When controlling for additional factors and addressing potential sample selection issues, we find the disparities between partisan and nonpartisan elections are still prevalent. For a typical respondent, the probability of rolling off in a nonpartisan election is 0.131. The comparable figures for partisan and quasi-partisan elections are 0.043 and 0.040, respectively. This confirms in large measure the finding that nonpartisan election formats decrease participation in elections (e.g., Bonneau and Hall 2009; Hall and Bonneau 2008). Interestingly, in this "typical" case, voter participation is essentially the same in partisan elections and quasi-partisan elections.

Beyond the election format, several individual-level factors exert statistically and substantively significant influence on roll-off in judicial elections. For example, we find that incumbency exerts a surprisingly strong influence on roll-off. While one may expect that citizens know somewhat more about an incumbent and thus may be less likely to roll-off in an election with an incumbent, incumbents may also enjoy structural advantages in the election that make the race less competitive and therefore less interesting to voters. Our results are more consistent with the latter explanation, with the probability of roll-off being about 0.06 higher in races with an incumbent than in open-seat races.

Respondents with college degrees have predicted probabilities of roll-off about 0.04 lower than those without college degrees, showing that education is not only a factor that drives individuals to the polls but that it also plays a role in whether they complete the entire ballot. Homeownership and weekly church attendance are statistically significant, though their effects are relatively modest, with homeowners having a reduction in the probability of roll-off of about 0.035 and union membership diminishing the probability of roll-off by about 0.01. Race and gender do not exert significant effects on roll-off rates in either year of our analyses.

Neither challenger quality nor per capita campaign spending came out as significant in 2012. We suspect this is due to the relatively small number (twenty) of elections we observe in 2012; with a larger set of elections we believe the effects we expected would be observable. In 2010, the results are similar except that spending is significant in the direction opposite to our expectations (higher roll-off is associated with more spending), though when one considers the magnitude in actual dollar terms of a one-unit change in per capita spending, the substantive effect of the variable becomes relatively trivial. We anticipate that as additional years of individual-level data become available, one may observe significant effects on these variables.

Conclusion

Ultimately, we find strong and clear support for the hypothesis that the presence of partisan labels increases voter participation. The simple, concise voting cue enables citizens to make an "on-the-fly" judgment about candidates in down-ballot races (like judicial elections) where citizens might not otherwise have much information about the candidates. Even quasi-partisan elections, where candidates are nominated by parties but the party affiliation is not listed on the ballot, have higher levels of participation relative to nonpartisan elections. Removing partisanship from the ballot reduces the pool of voters who feel adequately informed to cast a ballot. This finding is consistent with prior aggregate-level studies of this issue (Bonneau and Hall 2009; Dubois 1979).

Additionally, it is by no means clear that eliminating voters who rely solely on the partisan ballot's explicit partisan cues to inform their vote that nonpartisan elections genuinely remove the partisan element from elections. In the next chapter we evaluate the extent to which voters' party ID is a significant predictor of vote choice even in nonpartisan judicial elections.

Beyond providing a clearer portrait of the effect of the partisan election format on participation in judicial elections, we also provide some unique insight on the individual characteristics that affect participation in judicial elections. Because of the ecological fallacy, it is difficult to draw meaningful conclusions about the effect of individual-level characteristics on participation with the aggregate-level data on which existing studies of participation in judicial elections are based. This chapter not only allows us to confirm the canonical finding that education increases turnout, but also to demonstrate that more educated individuals are more likely to vote in down-ballot judicial elections once they have already come to the polling place. Our results clearly show that there is meaningful nonrandom variation in participation at the level of the individual voter, and that no portrait of participation in judicial elections is complete without accounting for the variation at the individual level.

The analysis above has several normative implications for those interested in the politics of electoral reform. It suggests that while individual factors such as education and connections to the community (being a homeowner) or even race-specific factors (the presence of an incumbent) can have an effect on participation, the largest factor is the structure of the ballot. Moving away from including partisanship on the ballot leads to lower levels of participation.

In this chapter, our focus has been on understanding individuals' decisions to participate in state supreme court elections. This is a matter of considerable importance because if certain types of individuals do not vote, the views of individuals like them will not be reflected in election outcomes. Nevertheless, one's choice of for whom to vote is at least as important as the choice regarding whether to vote. Accordingly, in the next chapter we turn our attention to the factors that determine for whom an individual casts his or her ballot.

2

VOTE CHOICE IN STATE SUPREME COURT ELECTIONS

As much as 80% of the electorate is completely unfamiliar with its candidates for judicial office.
—Charles Gardner Geyh, "Why Judicial Elections Stink"

In this chapter, we turn our attention from the determinants of participation to the determinants of vote choice. If most voters are completely unfamiliar with judicial candidates as some have claimed, then voting in these elections should be random, and we should not be able to explain individuals' vote choices by such variables as partisanship, ideology, qualifications of the candidates, and so forth. However, it may be the case that voters make decisions in judicial elections in much the same way they do in other elections. That is, while they may be somewhat unfamiliar with the candidates (a charge that can be leveled against many elective offices), voters may be familiar enough with them to behave in predictable and logical ways.

Although we discuss several factors that could determine vote choice, we focus primarily on the role of partisanship. At least since the publication of *The American Voter,* party identification has stood out as one of the most important factors, if not the single most important factor, in models of voting behavior in the American public (A. Campbell et al. 1960). Partisanship is a critically important heuristic for voters because it provides simple meaningful cues for complex political decisions (Kam 2005) and is relevant to a wide range of political choices (Huckfeldt et al. 1999). While our understanding of the role of partisanship in electoral behavior continues to go through expansions and refinements, it is clear that partisanship is a critically important part of understanding political behavior in the United States.

While it is difficult to overstate the importance of party identification in the political behavior literature, there is a large set of elections to which the applicability of partisanship is questionable: those that are nominally nonpartisan. While elections for national office and many state offices are traditional partisan elections, about three-fourths of municipal elections are nonpartisan (DeSantis and Renner 1991), as are those for many judges, school board officers, and even the Nebraska state legislature. These elections are conducted in the same manner as partisan elections (contested elections between multiple candidates), with the sole exception that the candidates' respective partisan affiliations are not listed on the ballot. Adrian (1959) found that over half of elections in the United States are nonpartisan in format. While some important work has been done on nonpartisan elections (e.g., Adrian 1959; Squire and Smith 1988; Schaffner, Streb, and Wright 2001), we know much less about voting behavior in these elections than in partisan elections.

The nonpartisan format has a long history in judicial elections. Progressives started arguing for removing party labels for judges around 1900 (Bonneau and Hall 2009). Currently, fifteen states elect their judges for their court of last resort using nonpartisan ballots, compared to only seven that use partisan elections (and three of those seven combine partisan elections for a judge to initially obtain a seat on the bench with retention elections for judges to retain their jobs).

In the context of judicial elections, the debate on partisan versus nonpartisan election formats has become particularly salient in the past decade. Although a spate of states have switched from contestable elections to a "merit" plan (which involves appointment and retention elections instead of competitive elections), since the late twentieth century the momentum behind the merit plan movement has stalled, as seen in the failure of recent bids to move to a merit plan in Nevada and Minnesota and with a recent constitutional amendment on the ballot in Tennessee that eliminated their version of the merit plan. However, since 2000 there has been interest in shifting from a contestable partisan election system to a contestable nonpartisan system, with Arkansas (2000) and North Carolina (2002) shifting from partisan to nonpartisan elections. Given the high degree of public support for judicial elections (see, for example, Geyh 2003; Bonneau and Hall 2009), nonpartisan elections are often seen as a viable reform for those who want to remove overt partisanship from the judicial selection process (see Carlton 2003; Schotland 2003; Berkowitz and Clay 2006).

Even though questions regarding judicial selection are becoming more important, only limited individual-level data exist to facilitate our understanding of the role partisanship plays in voters' decisions in judicial elections. Resolving this issue can potentially contribute to our understanding of voting behavior in judicial elections specifically and the relative effects of partisanship on voting in partisan and nonpartisan elections more generally. In this chapter, we use individual-level data from the 2010 and 2012 CCES to examine the effects of partisanship on vote choices in judicial elections. These data allow us to ascertain whether voters in nonpartisan elections (which are designed to remove—or at least reduce—partisanship) behave in similar ways to voters in partisan elections. Moreover, we are also able to determine whether characteristics such as education or campaign spending, which have been found to affect vote totals at the aggregate level, also affect individual vote choices.

Partisanship in Elections

Schaffner, Streb, and Wright (2001) characterize the debate over partisanship in elections as a clash between the progressives of the early twentieth century and a group of mid-twentieth-century political scientists led most prominently by Schattschneider (1942). Progressives saw the parties as the driving force behind political machines and thus sought to excise party politics from local elections, thereby dismantling machines and facilitating government responsiveness to the citizenry. Progressives argued that there was little connection between national party priorities and effective local governance, and that civically oriented citizens were fully capable of evaluating local candidates' platforms on local issues in the absence of partisan cues.

In contrast to the progressives, a strong movement in mid-twentieth-century political science argued that strong political parties were an important part of a well-functioning, healthy democratic system (Schattschneider 1942; American Political Science Association 1950). Individual citizens tend to be poorly informed about politics and therefore find that the benefits of participating tend to be outweighed by the costs of becoming informed and participating (Downs 1957). As such, a simple but effective cue like party identification allows voters to make rational choices in a cost-effective manner (Aldrich 1995; Page and Shapiro 1992). Removing partisan cues, then, may reduce rates of electoral participation and make it more difficult for those voters who do turn out to cast their ballots in a manner consistent with their political interests.

In the instance of judicial elections, the rationale is slightly different for removing partisanship from the ballot than for the progressives. While there was some concern about party machines controlling the judicial selection process, proponents of nonpartisan judicial elections argue that this scheme allows voters to hold judges accountable for their decisions and behavior on the bench "while insulating judges from the vagaries and vicissitudes of partisan tides" (Bonneau and Hall 2009, 8). Additionally, advocates of nonpartisan elections "hoped that more qualified jurists would be elected to the bench and that voters would make judgments based on the objective qualifications of the candidates instead of partisan tides" (Bonneau and Hall 2009, 8). That is, nonpartisan elections would maintain the benefits of elections (accountability) while at the same time improving the quality of the bench and ensuring that judges were not defeated only because of their party affiliation.[1]

Although both proponents and detractors of the nonpartisan format offer logical normative claims in support of their positions, the empirical evidence on the information voters actually use is limited and somewhat conflicted. In local elections, the results are fairly clear and consistent. In a study of nonpartisan school board elections, Berry and Howell (2007) control for partisanship among a large number of predictors of vote choice and find that partisanship is not a significant predictor of election outcomes. Similarly, a study of both mayoral and state legislative elections finds that removing partisanship from the ballot essentially eliminates the relationship between voters' party identifications and their vote choices (Schaffner, Streb, and Wright 2001). The primary limitation on these findings is that mayoral and state legislative races are often low-profile, low-cost, and low-information affairs. The ability of citizens to bring their party identification to bear on voting decisions may be different in contexts where, like state supreme court elections, there is a significant amount of money spent and there is more information circulating about the candidates. We suspect that the significant campaigning that defines contemporary judicial elections may generate cues that allow partisanship to enter voters' decision-making processes to at least some extent, even in nonpartisan elections.

Empirical results on the effect of nonpartisan election format on vote choice in judicial elections are both more scant than on local elections and also less consistent. In a study of nonpartisan judicial retention elections in California, Squire and Smith (1988) found that party identification had no significant effect on support for incumbents in retention elections, but that when voters were supplied with information about the party of the appointing governor (something akin to the judges' partisanship), voters' partisanship became a strong predictor of support for retention. This suggests that nonpartisan formats effectively achieve judicial reformers' goals of eliminating partisanship from the ballot.

However, several recent studies by Baum and various colleagues suggest that in Ohio, where party affiliations of state supreme court candidates do not appear on the general election ballot, party identification tends to have a strong effect on vote choice, particularly in highly visible campaigns (Baum and Klein 2007; Rock and Baum 2010). These works suggest that partisanship is still a key consideration in voters' decisions even in nonpartisan elections.

This view is consistent with the notion that partisanship in the contemporary era, while still involving a traditional component of self-identity (Green, Palmquist, and Schickler 2002), is primarily based on an ideological component (Fiorina 2002; Levendusky 2009). Indeed, Highton and Kam (2011) show that in recent years, voters have increasingly chosen their partisanship on the basis of their issue positions. If voters use issue positions to determine their own partisanship, we posit that if a sufficient amount of ideological issue content circulates in a nonpartisan election, voters may determine candidates' partisanship and apply their own party identification when casting ballots. We suspect that in state supreme court elections this is often the case.

Perhaps one explanation for the divergent findings in the judicial elections literature is that there are a number of limitations to these existing studies of vote choice in judicial elections. None of them examines vote choice in more than a single state, and both of the states examined in these studies have peculiarities that make generalization difficult. California uses retention elections (a simple up or down vote to retain an incumbent who faces no opponent), but it may only be in contestable nonpartisan elections that rival candidates have incentives to reveal enough ideological information about themselves and their opponents to enable voters to cast ballots in a partisan manner. Ohio's nonpartisan elections have a unique partisan element in that even though party labels do not appear on the ballot judicial contests, candidates are selected in partisan primaries. As a consequence, political parties are deeply involved in the selection process, and candidates' partisanship circulates in the media, which provides a clear signal (to voters who can remember it) as to how to apply their individual partisanship to their vote choice.

Partisanship and Vote Choice in Judicial Elections

DATA

We draw our data from the 2010 and 2012 Cooperative Congressional Election Study (CCES).[2] As in the last chapter, we use the validated CCES so our data contain only those respondents who have been verified as actually voting in the election (as opposed to their self-reports). The 2010 and 2012 judicial elections are in many ways ideal for examination. In the 2010 election cycle, we observed seventeen contested elections across ten states, while the 2012 election brought fourteen contested races in ten states. The races used here differ slightly from those used in the last chapter because we cannot incorporate vote choice in multicandidate elections (held in West Virginia and Michigan) as easily in a binary choice model as we can turnout and also because some nonpartisan elections, while contested, involve only candidates of the same party affiliation.[3] A list of the races analyzed in this chapter can be found in appendix B.

The level of spending in the 2010 and 2012 judicial elections was consistent with the level of spending in judicial races in other recent midterm election cycles, though the amount of money spent on television advertising in the 2010 election was somewhat higher than other midterm election cycles (Skaggs et al. 2011). Given the levels of spending and advertising, we are confident that voters in the 2010 elections were exposed to judicial campaigns at a level that is typical for judicial elections since the year 2000. Across these thirty-one elections we have a wide range of states and regions represented in the data.

Given some slight differences in the way the data were collected, we analyze the 2010 and 2012 election data separately. In the 2010 election, the judicial vote choice questions were not asked of all CCES respondents in states with the contested elections. Instead, the vote choice question was placed on three modules of one thousand respondents. Because not all of the respondents on each module lived in states where there was a contestable judicial election, many respondents did not yield a response to a judicial vote choice question. However, respondents in states with multiple elections answered the vote choice question for each election in which they participated. In the 2012 election cycle, the judicial vote choice question was asked of all CCES respondents who lived in a state with a contested judicial election. However, due to time constraints on the survey, in states where there were multiple state supreme court elections, each respondent was asked the judicial vote choice question for only one randomly selected race (each respondent was asked about only one specific race, but all races in the state were covered), leading to only one vote choice per respondent being observed in the 2012 CCES. Nevertheless, because of the enormous sample size of the full CCES, our sample size for the 2012 elections is still many times larger than for the 2010 elections. Given the differences in sample sizes between the 2010 and 2012 CCES, we analyze the data separately for each year as we did in the previous chapter.

A FIRST LOOK AT THE DATA

Our primary goal in this chapter is to evaluate the extent to which partisanship affects vote choice in both partisan and nonpartisan elections. Our approach to that question begins quite simply: we can array the vote choices of CCES respondents by their party identification for both partisan and nonpartisan elections and evaluate how much more likely (if at all) Republicans are to vote Republican and Democrats are to vote Democrat. This process requires identifying the partisanship of candidates in nonpartisan elections. Identifying the partisanship of nonpartisan judicial candidates is a reasonably straightforward task and has been accomplished for a large number of candidates by previous scholars as part of a measure of ideology (Brace, Langer, and Hall 2001). We coded candidate partisanship by consulting their personal statements of partisanship, service in other elected positions in government, service in government that required appointment by partisan officials, service in state or local party organizations, and, in one case, declared membership in the "Tea Party."

Table 2.1 shows the relationship between vote choice and party identification in partisan and nonpartisan elections for the smaller 2010 sample, whereas table 2.2 arrays the results for the larger 2012 sample.[4]

Political scientists have long understood the strong influence that partisanship exerts in partisan elections for both the U.S. presidency and Congress (e.g., A. Campbell et al. 1960; Keith et al. 1992). Finding a substantial effect of partisanship in partisan judicial elections, then, is unsurprising. While the effect is clear and strong in 2010 (about 70% of Republicans voting for the Republican judicial candidate and nearly 80% of Democrats voting for the Democratic candidate), the effect is particularly strong in the larger 2012 partisan judicial elections, with about 95% of Republicans and Democrats alike voting for the candidate who shares their party identification. What is more striking, though, is the pronounced influence of partisanship in nonpartisan judicial elections. In our 2010 election sample, the effect of partisanship was about as strong in nonpartisan elections (about 80% of Republicans voting Republican and about 60% of Democrats voting Democrat in nonpartisan elections) as the partisan elections held that year. While the effect of partisanship in the 2012 sample was not as large in nonpartisan elections as it was in partisan elections, the effect of partisanship is still clear with nearly 80% of Republicans and over 70% of Democrats voting for their party's candidate. These figures cast doubt on the conventional wisdom that nonpartisan elections eliminate partisan considerations when voters are called upon to select or retain judges.[5]

TABLE 2.1 Partisanship and vote choice in the 2010 state supreme court elections by election format

	PARTISAN ELECTIONS (%)			NONPARTISAN ELECTIONS (%)		
	REPUBLICAN	INDEPENDENT	DEMOCRAT	REPUBLICAN	INDEPENDENT	DEMOCRAT
Vote Republican	69.0	75.9	21.3	80.2	23.5	39.7
Vote Democrat	31.0	24.1	78.7	19.8	76.5	60.3

Note: Data from the 2010 CCES, $n = 361$. For partisan elections the design-based $F = 3.999$, $p < 0.05$. For nonpartisan elections, the design-based $F = 16.314$, $p < 0.05$.

TABLE 2.2 Partisanship and vote choice in the 2012 state supreme court elections by election format

	PARTISAN ELECTIONS (%)			NONPARTISAN ELECTIONS (%)		
	REPUBLICAN	INDEPENDENT	DEMOCRAT	REPUBLICAN	INDEPENDENT	DEMOCRAT
Vote Republican	94.6	64.6	4.4	79.1	59.6	29.5
Vote Democrat	5.4	35.4	95.6	20.9	40.4	70.5

Note: Data from the 2012 CCES, $n = 4{,}816$. For partisan elections the design-based $F = 308.12$, $p < 0.05$. For nonpartisan elections, the design-based $F = 143.93$, $p < 0.05$.

The results in tables 2.1 and 2.2 are strongly suggestive that partisanship plays an important role in voters' decisions not only in partisan elections, but also in nonpartisan elections. There are a number of limitations on this analysis. First, while the crosstabs allow us to test the significance of the effect of party identification within the realm of partisan and nonpartisan election formats, respectively, we lack a test of whether the effect of party identification differs statistically across election formats. Moreover, the crosstabular tests, while simple to interpret, do not control for additional factors known to influence vote choice that may also be correlated with party identification or election format. As such, we move to a more sophisticated and more fully specified discrete choice model of vote choice in state supreme court elections.

Discrete Choice Model of Vote Choice

For our discrete choice model of vote choice, we employ a probit estimator with vote choice (1 = Democratic vote, 0 = Republican vote) as the dependent variable.[6] Our primary independent variable of interest is respondents' party identifications, coded 1 for Democrats, −1 for Republicans, and 0 for independents. To allow the effect of partisanship to vary across partisan and nonpartisan election formats, we include a dichotomous variable for a partisan election format (1 = partisan, 0 = nonpartisan) and an interaction term between party identification and election format.

We also include a number of additional control variables. The power of incumbency tends to be strong in elections generally (Cover 1977; Abramowitz and Segal 1992; Mayhew 2008) as well as in state supreme court elections specifically (Bonneau and Hall 2009). As such, we include a variable for accounting for the party with the incumbency advantage in the vote choice the respondent is considering, with 1 denoting a Democratic incumbent, −1 denoting a Republican incumbent, and 0 denoting a race with no incumbent (an open seat).[7] We also include controls for a variety of demographic factors that have been shown at times to influence vote choice, including gender (Alvarez and Nagler 1995), race (Ansolabehere, Persily, and Stewart 2010), and educational attainment (Kenny 1998; Burbank 1997). We also include a variable for whether respondents identify themselves as "born-again" Christians. This is in part because of the general influence of religion on vote choice (Layman 1997), but also due to the increased use of both overt signaling of candidates' religious affiliations and more subtle religious undertones (claims of being a "family values" judge), both of which might activate an individual's partisanship in an electoral setting (Campbell, Green, and Layman 2011). We also include an interaction between election format and each of these control variables to account for the possibility that the controls may matter more (or less) in nonpartisan elections where voters may lack partisan cues (Schaffner, Streb, and Wright 2001). For the 2010 election model, standard errors are clustered by respondent because respondents in some states have more than one vote choice (e.g., they voted in more than one race because their state had multiple state high court elections); in the 2012 election each voter was randomly assigned to answer the vote choice question for only one state supreme court election if their state had multiple contests for the high court, and clustered standard errors are therefore unnecessary.

Results of the model estimation appear in table 2.3. While there are a number of differences between the results for the 2010 election and those for the 2012 election, there is a key similarity that is consistent with the results from the crosstabs above: there is a strong, clear influence of partisanship in both partisan and nonpartisan judicial elections. Given the complexity of interpreting an interaction term in a nonlinear model, rather than dwelling on the signs and significance of the probit coefficients, we present some discrete changes in the probability of voting for the Democratic state supreme court candidate in figure 2.1. To calculate the discrete changes displayed in the figure, we found the probability of voting for the Democratic candidate for a Democratic voter who was participating in a partisan election in which there is no incumbent, and gender, race, education, and religion are held constant at their modal values. Then we calculated the probability for an identical situation except we switched the voter's party identification to Republican. This difference represents the discrete change in the probability of voting for the Democratic candidate for changing the voter's party identification from Democrat to Republican in a partisan election. We then repeat the analogous computation for a nonpartisan election.

In the 2010 election, we observe no statistically significant dif-

TABLE 2.3 Probit models of vote choice in the 2010 and 2012 state supreme court elections

	2010 CCES		2012 CCES	
	COEFFICIENT	STANDARD ERROR	COEFFICIENT	STANDARD ERROR
Party ID	0.611*	0.130	0.637*	0.045
Partisan format	−0.217	0.665	0.564*	0.226
Party ID × Partisan format	−0.006	0.267	0.994*	0.099
Incumbency	−0.101	0.118	0.097	0.059
Incumbency × Partisan format	−0.469	0.366	−0.019	0.101
College	−0.078	0.237	0.280*	0.077
College × Partisan Format	0.458	0.430	−0.305*	0.154
White	−0.098	0.338	−0.021	0.112
White × Partisan format	0.206	0.467	−0.313	0.226
Male	−0.086	0.240	−0.101	0.078
Male × Partisan format	0.070	0.418	−0.117	0.171
Born again	0.180	0.274	−0.132	0.090
Born again × Partisan format	−0.889	0.427	−0.125	0.177
Constant	0.282	0.400	−0.059	0.124
n	361		4816	
χ^2	111.32 ($p < 0.001$)		819.74 ($p < 0.001$)	
McKelvey/Zavoina r^2	0.169		0.588	

Note: Data from the 2010 and 2012 CCES studies. *$p < 0.05$, two-tailed.

ference in the effect of party identification on vote choice. This is due in part to the relatively small differences in the point estimates of the effects, but also due to the substantial uncertainty around the point estimates (likely caused by the relatively small sample size available in the 2010 CCES). In the larger 2012 CCES sample, there are clear and statistically significant differences in the relative effects of party identification on vote choice between partisan and nonpartisan elections, with a change in party ID from Republican to Democrat resulting in an increase of about 0.47 in the probability of a Democratic vote. In contrast, the same change in party ID under a partisan election format is estimated to cause a 0.88 increase in the probability of a Democratic vote.

While there are clear differences in the magnitude of the effect of party identification on vote choice across partisan and nonpartisan election formats, it is equally clear that partisanship also exerts strong and meaningful effects on the outcome of nonpartisan elections. Although partisanship's effect may be somewhat attenuated in nonpartisan elections, it is far from eliminated.

None of the control variables in the 2010 election model are statistically significant, again perhaps due to the relatively small sample size (and in the instance of incumbency, perhaps due to the general anti-incumbent sentiment that prevailed in the 2010 elections). However, in the 2012 model where the placement of the judicial vote choice question on the common content of the CCES facilitated a

FIGURE 2.1. Discrete changes in the probability of voting for the Democrat due to a shift in party identification

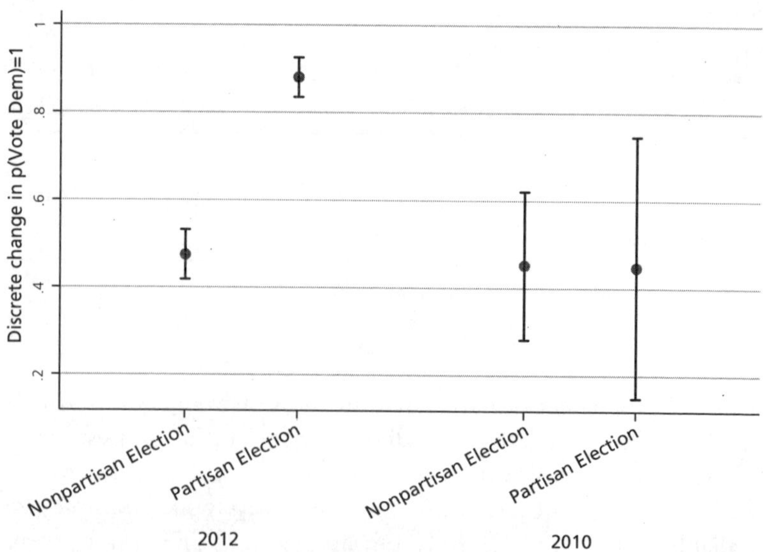

Note: Predicted probabilities based on the model in table 2.3.

substantially larger sample size, we were able to detect effects for several of the control variables. Specifically, individuals with a college education have a modestly higher probability of voting Democratic in nonpartisan elections, but the interaction of college and partisan format suggests that any effects in nonpartisan elections wash out in partisan elections. We find no statistically significant effects for incumbency, race, gender, or self-identification as a born-again Christian.

In short, the bivariate findings suggesting a strong influence of partisanship in nonpartisan elections are borne out by the more complicated model. Nevertheless, we pursue a number of additional extensions and robustness checks on these findings, specifically the influences of campaign intensity and ideology.

What about Campaign Intensity?

While many nonpartisan elections may be intense enough to facilitate the determination of a candidate's party identification, it is possible that in lower-intensity elections voters may lack the information necessary for identification of the candidate's party ID in nonpartisan elections (see, for example, Rock and Baum 2010). On the other hand, it may be that even lower intensity nonpartisan state supreme court elections still allow enough information to circulate to allow individuals to discern the ideology of the candidates.

To address this possibility, we use the total amount of campaign spending in each race as a measure of campaign intensity. We then rerun the models from table 2.3 also adding campaign spending and interacting it in a three way interaction with the respondent's party identification and the election format of the election. This enables us to evaluate whether the difference in rates of partisan voting between partisan and nonpartisan voting is conditional on the level of campaign spending. Results from the model estimation appear in table 2.4.

Our primary interest for the purposes of this chapter is in the effect of party identification across different election formats in either low- , median- , or high-spending elections. Particularly with a three-way interaction, identifying the right comparisons is somewhat more involved than a simple examination of the statistical significance (consider Ai and Norton 2003). As such, we take

TABLE 2.4 Spending, partisanship, election format, and vote choice in the 2010 and 2012 state supreme court elections

	2010 CCES		2012 CCES	
	COEFFICIENT	STANDARD ERROR	COEFFICIENT	STANDARD ERROR
Party ID	0.814*	0.280	0.536*	0.091
Partisan format	−0.822	0.768	0.172	0.284
Spending (in hundred thousands)	0.052	0.028	−0.020	0.013
Party ID × Partisan format	−0.368	0.407	1.162*	0.162
Spending × Partisan format	0.142*	0.050	0.059*	0.017
Party ID × Spending	0.016	0.028	0.014	0.012
Party ID × Partisan format × Spending	0.053	0.056	−0.028	0.016
Incumbency	−0.047	0.117	0.162*	0.071
Incumbency × Partisan format	−0.515	0.384	−0.223	0.115
College	−0.052	0.239	0.282*	0.077
College × Partisan format	0.449	0.429	−0.326*	0.155
White	0.158	0.353	−0.026	0.112
White × Partisan format	−0.115	0.557	−0.425	0.238
Male	−0.171	0.253	−0.112	0.078
Male × Partisan format	0.125	0.424	−0.122	0.176
Born again	0.214	0.262	−0.130	0.090
Born again × Partisan format	−0.954	0.537	−0.234	0.186
Constant	0.148	0.543	0.123	0.166
n	361		4816	
χ^2	107.37 ($p < 0.01$)		846.72 ($p < 0.01$)	
McKelvey/Zavoina r^2	0.292		0.609	

Note: Data from the 2010 and 2012 CCES studies. *$p < 0.05$, two-tailed.

a moment to describe the comparisons we seek to make. The comparison of primary interest begins with calculating the predicted probability of voting for the Democratic judicial candidate for a Democrat respondent in a partisan election with low levels of campaign spending (we choose the minimum observed value in our data) and all other variables set to their modal values. Then we calculate the predicted probability for an identical respondent with the exception of being a Republican. The difference between those two predicted probabilities is the discrete change in the probability of voting for the Democratic candidate associated with a change in party identification from Republican to Democrat (for a partisan election with low levels of campaign spending). We then repeat this process calculating a discrete change in the probability of voting for the Democratic candidate for a Republican versus a Democrat respondent but in a nonpartisan election (though still with low levels of campaign spending). The difference between these two discrete changes then tells us how different the effect of party identification is on vote choice in a partisan versus a nonpartisan election. By repeating this entire calculation of differences in discrete changes for median levels of spending and high levels of spending (in our case, the maximum observed level of campaign spending in 2010), we can compare whether difference in the effect of party ID on vote choice between partisan and nonpartisan election formats is conditional on the level of spending in the race.

To be sure, the differences in the discrete changes, like any statistic, carry some measure of uncertainty around them. Popular methods for addressing complex interactions have recently focused on simulation techniques (Brambor, Clark, and Golder 2006). We use the popular "Clarify" software (King, Tomz, and Wittenberg 2000) to simulate the difference in discrete changes in predicted probabilities for partisan and nonpartisan elections across different levels of spending.[8] We present these differences in discrete changes in figure 2.2.

In the 2010 elections, there are no significant differences observed between partisan and nonpartisan elections at any level of spending. With the much larger 2012 sample, we do observe statistically significant differences in discrete changes (due to partisanship) across partisan and nonpartisan elections, but these differences are present at every level of spending. The difference in the differences in discrete changes between high-spending and low-spending elections is not statistically significant, however, suggesting that lower levels of spending neither exacerbate nor attenuate the differences in the effect of party identification on vote choice between partisan and nonpartisan elections.[9] We do note, however, that the effect of incumbency, which narrowly missed statistical significance in the model presented in table 2.3, is statistically significant when spending is included, suggesting support for the notion that sitting judges enjoy at least a modest incumbency advantage. This advantage, however, is not conditional on ballot format.

What about Political Ideology?

Finally, while we have focused primarily on partisanship, one may also wonder about the effect of ideology on voting decisions. Like many, we conceive of contemporary partisanship as primarily reflecting the ideological cleavages in society. This may be caused by polarization in the electorate (Abramowitz and Saunders 1998) or

FIGURE 2.2. Differences in the effect of partisanship in partisan and nonpartisan elections as spending varies

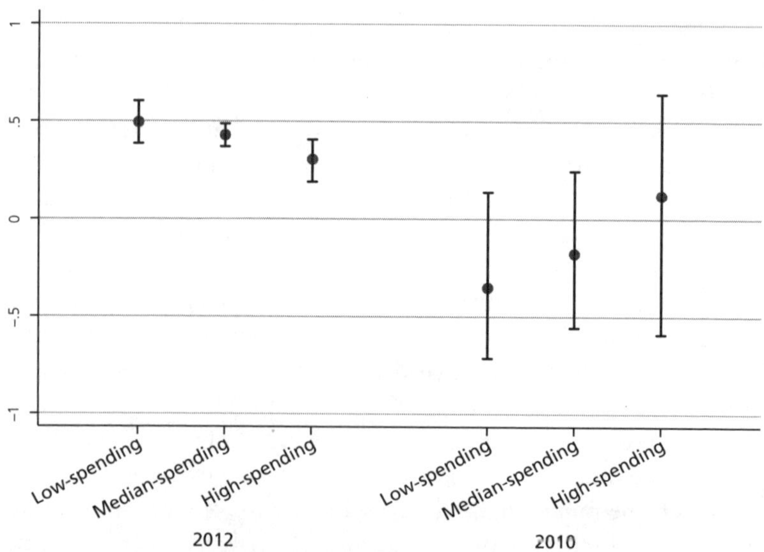

Note: Predicted probabilities based on the model in table 2.4.

instead because elite polarization has clarified the meaning of ideological labels (Levine, Carmines, and Huckfeldt 1997; Hinich and Munger 1997), which in turn has led to the sorting of voters into parties on the basis of ideology even without ideological polarization in the mass public (Levendusky 2009). In either case, the foregoing analysis is based on the premise that controlling for ideology is unnecessary because it represents the same conceptual divisions in society as partisanship. Nevertheless, one may hold that the electorate is still not fully "sorted" into parties on the basis of ideology or that partisanship still reflects significant considerations apart from ideology. Thus, controlling for ideology in addition to partisanship may make sense. Before moving to the next chapter, we undertake such an analysis here.

For proponents of nonpartisan elections, the goal of removing partisan labels is to depoliticize elections and instead focus on the qualifications and aptitude of judges. If nonpartisan elections were shown to be influenced as heavily by ideology as partisan elections, it would call the effectiveness of nonpartisan elections into question. In addition, controlling for ideology allows us to determine whether our prior finding (that the effects of partisanship are still robust under a nonpartisan election format) is robust. We re-estimate the model with full controls presented in table 2.3 above and include ideology (as measured by the standard seven-point liberal-conservative scale) and the interaction of ideology and election format. The results of these models appear in table 2.5, and figure 2.3 depicts the discrete change in the probability of voting for the Democratic candidate due to a shift in ideology from strong conservative to strong liberal (holding partisanship constant at independent, incumbency constant at no incumbent, and all other values at their modal values).

For the smaller 2010 sample, once we control for ideology the effect of partisanship becomes statistically insignificant. The coefficients suggest that if anything, ideology has a slightly weaker effect in partisan elections, though that difference in effect size is not statistically significant. In the larger 2012 sample, the effect of ideology is also strong and significant, though the effect of partisanship remains consistent with the 2012 results without the ideological control variable. Notably, as in the 2010 sample, the effect of ideology does not differ across election formats in the 2012 sample. In short, the use of

TABLE 2.5 Ideology, election format, and vote choice in the 2010 and 2012 state supreme court elections

	2010 CCES		2012 CCES	
	COEFFICIENT	STANDARD ERROR	COEFFICIENT	STANDARD ERROR
Party ID	0.025	0.197	0.424*	0.065
Partisan format	1.095	0.835	0.295	0.367
Party ID × Partisan format	0.507	0.365	0.934*	0.121
Ideology	0.427*	0.119	0.173*	0.035
Ideology × Partisan format	−0.380	0.203	0.067	0.104
Incumbency	−0.011	0.113	0.096	0.059
Incumbency × Partisan format	−0.560	0.360	−0.065	0.100
College	−0.215	0.233	0.237*	0.079
College × Partisan format	0.580	0.438	−0.242	0.163
White	−0.113	0.315	−0.013	0.113
White × Partisan format	0.345	0.532	−0.301	0.222
Male	−0.017	0.217	−0.103	0.079
Male × Partisan format	0.028	0.420	−0.159	0.178
Born again	0.556*	0.261	−0.056	0.091
Born again × Partisan format	−1.243*	0.491	−0.127	0.208
Constant	−0.770	0.492	−0.693*	0.185
n	360		4721	
χ^2	109.26 ($p < 0.001$)		850.76 ($p < 0.01$)	
McKelvey/Zavoina r^2	0.249		0.613	

Note: Data from the 2010 and 2012 CCES studies. *$p < 0.05$, two-tailed. The sample sizes in these estimates decline slightly from those in tables 2.3 and 2.4 due to missing values in the CCES on the ideology measure.

nonpartisan elections does not diminish the influence of ideological considerations among voters in judicial elections.

Conclusion

Party identification has long been held as the core determinant of voters' choices. However, the stated goal of nonpartisan elections, for better or for worse, is to remove voters' abilities to bring their partisan identification to bear on their voting decisions. Conventional wisdom holds that nonpartisan elections succeed in this goal. However, the results presented here reveal that nonpartisan elections are ineffective at achieving their stated goal in state supreme court elections. We suspect the same would hold true of nonpartisan elections in any context where campaign spending is high and a reasonable amount of information is available to voters. Although political science typically takes a dismal view of voters' capacities, these results suggest that voters are able to identify the partisan identification of candidates from ideological and issue-based cues even when

FIGURE 2.3. Discrete changes in the probability of voting for the Democrat due to a shift from strong conservative to strong liberal

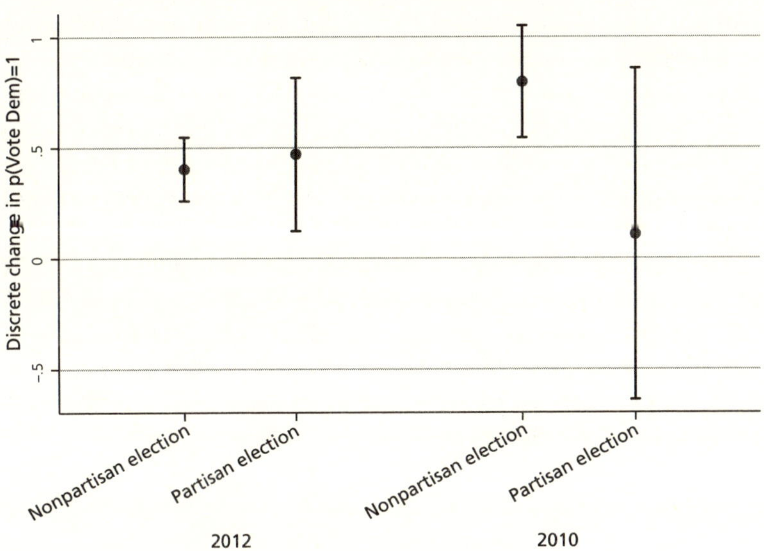

Note: Predicted probabilities based on the model in table 2.5.

candidates' explicit partisanship is omitted from the ballot. This may not have been easily accomplished in times past, when partisanship and ideology were more distinct dimensions of electoral choice (e.g., Rabinowitz, Gurian, and Macdonald 1984). However, the relatively recent sorting of candidates and voters into parties on the basis of ideology (Levendusky 2009) makes this task cognitively simpler. Additionally, more campaign spending and advertising in nonpartisan judicial elections (e.g., Bonneau and Hall 2009; Hall and Bonneau 2013) means that the cues voters need to infer candidate partisanship are widely available. When controlling for voter ideology in addition to party identification, we find that the effect of ideology does not vary across election formats, reinforcing the notion that nonpartisan elections do not mitigate the influence of political factors (such as partisanship and ideology) in judicial elections.

In addition to contributing to our understanding of partisanship in voting behavior, our results also have normative implications for the debate over methods of judicial selection. While some have argued that nonpartisan elections are more desirable than partisan elections, our individual-level analysis, combined with existing aggregate-level analysis, does not paint a flattering picture of nonpartisan elections in terms of their ability to mitigate the influence of partisanship in elections. Coupled with the results in chapter 1, our data demonstrate that nonpartisan elections lead to decreased voter participation but do not remove partisanship from the decision calculus of voters. Thus, this method of selection pays a heavy cost in terms of participation but does not reap the purported benefit of removing partisanship.

In the next chapter, we explore this further by conducting a series of laboratory experiments assessing how much partisan content is necessary for voters to behave in a partisan manner in nonpartisan elections. These experiments allow us to understand what types of information voters use to make decisions in elections, as well as how strong a signal candidates must send to voters.

3

VOTING DECISIONS IN PARTISAN AND NONPARTISAN ELECTIONS

By creating an artificial environment, a researcher can concisely measure how subtle changes in the environment impact outcomes. . . . All researchers would love to have total control over some naturally occurring environment (although such total control would mean the environment was not naturally occurring!), but this is almost always unfeasible. Consequently, the artificial nature of laboratory experiments allows researchers to mimic the naturally occurring environment with total controls to measure behavior within that environment.

—Kenneth C. Williams, *Introduction to Game Theory: A Behavioral Approach*

In the previous chapter, we found that nonpartisan elections are minimally effective at removing partisan cues from voters. While Democrats are somewhat likely to vote for the Democratic candidate (and Republicans are more likely to vote for the Republican candidate) in partisan elections than nonpartisan elections, there is still a remarkable amount of partisan voting in nonpartisan elections.

This finding is unique in many ways. Adamany and Dubois (1976) found that the correlation between partisanship and vote choice in nonpartisan elections in Wisconsin was rather weak in comparison to several partisan states. While some scholarship has shown higher rates of partisan voting than Adamany and Dubois found, those studies have often been focused on Ohio (e.g., Barber 1971; Rock and Baum 2010), which has a quasi-partisan system where parties can still nominate candidates even though party affiliation does not appear on the ballot. Some research has hinted at this finding (e.g., Dubois 1980; Kritzer 2007), though the results are limited to a handful of states or are inconsistent across states and elections examined. Further, those results are limited to crosstabular analyses that lack controls for additional factors.

While we consider the findings in chapter 2 to be sound, they have some limitations in common with other studies evaluating the correlation between partisanship and vote choice in judicial elections. Observational data like the CCES (or data brought to bear by Adamany and Dubois, Barber, Dubois, Kritzer, and Rock and Baum) can only take us so far because we cannot strictly control individuals' exposure to partisan and issue-oriented information about the candidates. Experimental data also allow us to hold everything about the election constant rather than dealing with electoral eccentricities across the sundry states. Thus, in this chapter, we make use of laboratory experiments to ascertain why partisan voting continues to be prevalent in nonpartisan elections. Our goal with the experiments presented here is simply to determine whether providing subjects in a carefully controlled lab experiment with candidates' issue positions and background allows subjects to correctly ascertain the party identification of the candidates. If so, then coupled with the results presented in chapter 2, we will have particularly persuasive evidence that nonpartisan elections are minimally effective at limiting the influence of partisanship in judicial elections.

Why Experiments?

Over the past decade, the experimental approach to studying politics has become a common method for studying politics (e.g., Morton and Williams 2010). Experiments allow scholars to randomly assign subjects to different treatment groups (and a control group) and vary their exposure to a key independent variable of interest. We use experiments to test the straightforward claim that the type of election (partisan versus nonpartisan) affects the choices voters make. There are two primary reasons why we engage in laboratory experiments in this case. First, our results in chapter 2 might be driven by extraneous factors for which we did not control. In an observational study, we can never be sure we have controlled for all relevant factors (though we use theory to guide us in selecting variables for inclusion). To the extent we have missed something important, our results might be spurious. Second, by randomly assigning subjects to treatment groups, we can isolate the specific effect of our independent variable of interest (type of election). The randomization process allows us to control for all other possible confounding factors (Kellstedt and Whitten 2013; Morton and Williams 2010; Williams 2013). Thus, if we find a relationship (or lack thereof) between the type of election and vote choice, our confidence that this relationship is real is quite high. This is why experiments are said to be high in internal validity.

Where experiments tend to be weaker is in external validity, or the extent to which we can generalize from our experiment to a larger population (Williams 2013). This is not a concern for us here because the CCES data analyzed in chapter 2 are generalizable. Thus, the combination of the external validity of the survey data and the internal validity of the experiment put us in excellent position to make generalizable causal claims about the relationship between type of election and vote choice, assuming the results complement each other. As we discuss below, we conduct multiple experiments with varying levels of information presented to subjects in order to uncover a possible causal relationship.

Experiment 1: Strong Partisan Information

Our first effort to determine the effects of partisan labels on rates of partisan voting uses information gleaned from real campaigns in partisan and nonpartisan elections. While this is information actually used, the partisan signals that the candidates are sending are pretty clear. Moreover, unlike in an actual campaign, the candidates' message does not have to cut through a lot of other campaign "clutter." Thus, we consider this a "strong partisan information" condition. In this experiment, the ads from the candidates are the only information voters have.

EXPERIMENT 1 DESCRIPTION

We recruited subjects from two introductory-level general education courses at a western university in the United States, one an introductory American politics course and the other an introductory economics course.[1] Both courses are primarily for non–political science majors and draw students from a wide range of majors from across the campus. Subjects assigned to the nonpartisan condition received a description of two candidates who were running for state supreme court. The descriptions, which appear in appendix C, outline the two candidates' legal backgrounds, qualifications, and their general views on several issues. The descriptions of the candidates' issue positions were based on statements made in recent judicial elections and information that was circulating during the campaign about the candidates, including claims that a candidate supports "traditional family values" and will "interpret the law rather than legislate from the bench" (for the judge who is a Republican but not named as such) or who is "strongly committed to individual rights" and will use the power of the judiciary to promote "equality and fairness" (for the judge who is a Democrat but not named as such). The information provided about candidates is comparable to information that judicial candidates circulate about themselves or to what routinely appears in interest group endorsements or voter guides.[2] Thus, our treatment has a high degree of ecological validity (Williams 2013, 33).

While we have made efforts to generate candidate descriptions that approximate the kind of information circulating about candidates in nonpartisan elections, diminished generalizability is a natural tradeoff with the high degree of internal validity an experimental design offers. We recognize, however, that in the course of a campaign, voters may not encounter all of these pieces of information and will not likely encounter them all at once immediately before casting their ballot. As such, it is important to interpret these results in tandem with the results based on the observational data in chapter 2. We also hasten to add that we are conducting these experiments to see whether, in a controlled environment, voters are able to use partisan cues independent of the party identification of the candidate on the ballot. We have already established that, in the actual election, voters in nonpartisan states can generally identify the candidate who shares their party identification. We are trying to uncover why this is the case in this chapter.

Subjects assigned to the partisan treatment received descriptions of the two candidates along with the candidates' respective party affiliations. Subjects in the nonpartisan treatment condition received the identical descriptions of the candidates as in partisan condition except the party affiliation of the candidates was not given. After reading the candidate descriptions, subjects in both conditions were asked which candidate they would vote for (or if they would abstain from voting in the race). Given that assignment to partisan or nonpartisan conditions was random and all other information was held constant, any differences in the rate of partisan voting between the two conditions can be attributed to the presence or absence of an explicit partisan cue in the candidate descriptions.[3] Additional details on the experimental protocol appear in appendix C.

EXPERIMENT 1 RESULTS

The dependent variable for the experimental data is subjects' revealed vote choice, coded 1 for the Democratic candidate and 0 for the Republican candidate (regardless of whether they are formally identified as such to subjects). We then use voter party identification (coded −1 for Republicans, 1 for Democrats, and 0 otherwise),[4] partisan versus nonpartisan format, and the interaction between the two as independent variables in a probit model. From the resulting coefficients, we can evaluate the effect of party identification on vote choice and formally test the extent to which the effects of party identification vary across partisan and nonpartisan conditions. The estimation results appear in table 3.1.

The results show a strong effect of party identification on vote choice, but there is no statistically significant difference in the magnitude effect of party identification on vote choice across partisan and nonpartisan election formats. For a subject in the partisan condition, shifting from a Republican to a Democratic party identification increases the probability of a Democratic vote choice by 0.747 with a 95% confidence interval of (0.615, 0.879). For a subject in the nonpartisan condition, shifting from a Republican to a Democratic Party identification increases the probability of a Democratic vote choice by 0.627 with a 95% confidence interval of (0.480, 0.772). The difference between these effects is not statistically significant ($p = 0.232$).

These experimental results show that in the face of clear and rela-

TABLE 3.1 Probit model of vote choice in experiment 1

VARIABLE	COEFFICIENT (STANDARD ERROR)
Party ID	0.962* (0.135)
Partisan format	0.256 (0.187)
Party ID × Partisan format	0.192 (0.204)
Constant	−0.398 (0.126)
χ^2	127.09 ($p < 0.001$)
McKelvey/Zavoina r^2	0.438
% Correctly Predicted	84.5%
PRE	0.438
n	323

Note: *$p < 0.05$

tively strong information about candidates, voters can easily translate candidate statements into partisan language, making clear that in the presence of strong signals about issue positions, explicit use of partisanship is unnecessary to facilitate partisan voting. Voters in nonpartisan elections can use information presented over the course of the campaign to identify the partisan identification of candidates. Nevertheless, given that the partisan signals may not always be as strong as those in this experiment, we conducted a second round of experiments using more subtle partisan cues.

Experiment 2: Subtle Partisan Information

While candidates regularly make statements of the type we used in our vignette above, not all candidate statements send as clear of an ideological signal as the ones we used above. Candidates may be somewhat more measured in their claims in some instances, and those muted statements may not have the same effect on individuals as the more overt ideological statements we tested in the experiment above. Additionally, the clutter of campaigns may mute strong partisan signals even when they are sent. This being the case, we ask whether the partisanship exerts the same influence in nonpartisan elections when the experimental cues regarding candidates' issue positions are more subtle.

EXPERIMENT 2 DESCRIPTION

In experiment 1, we held the description of the candidates constant and varied only whether the candidates' partisan affiliations were explicitly revealed. In experiment 2 we again vary whether the candidates' partisan affiliations are explicitly revealed, but we do so across two different descriptions of the candidates. In the first description of the candidates, voters receive descriptions of the background and qualifications of the candidates as in experiment 1, but they receive only a brief and subtle hint as to the candidates' partisanship. Specifically, the Republican candidate is described as believing "judges should interpret the law rather than legislate from the bench" and the Democrat is described as believing "judges should use the power of the judiciary to promote equality and fairness in society." The descriptions for the candidates are presented both with and without explicitly identifying the partisanship of the candidates.

In the second description of the candidates, subjects receive the same description of the candidates' background and qualifications as in the first description, but they do not receive even the subtle hint, instead being told that the judge "promises to decide cases fairly and behave with integrity" for the Republican candidate and that the Democratic candidate "promises to treat all who come before him equally and behave professionally." In the nonpartisan condition, these descriptions of the candidates are presented without identifying the partisanship of the candidates, while the partisan condition explicitly reveals the partisanship of the candidates. These manipulations allow us to determine whether partisanship still exerts a measure of influence in nonpartisan elections as the amount of issue or ideological content in the candidate descriptions is more limited than in the vignettes used in experiment 1. The full text of the vignettes can be found in appendix C.

As with experiment 1, subjects for experiment 2 were also recruited from a large introductory level general education course at the same western university as experiment 1. The experiments were conducted about nine months apart. The course subjects were drawn from was a general education course in U.S. institutions that covered basic aspects of U.S. history, economics, and American politics. As with the courses used in experiment 1, this course is primarily for non–political science majors and draws students from the full spectrum of higher education majors.

EXPERIMENT 2 RESULTS

As with our previous analysis, we code vote choice as 1 for a Democratic vote and 0 for a Republican vote. Subjects' party affiliations remain the independent variable of primary interest. However, the effect of party affiliation may vary across the four experimental prompts (no partisan information in the vignette, nonpartisan format; no partisan information in the vignette, partisan format; subtle partisan information in the vignette, partisan format; subtle partisan information in the vignette, nonpartisan format). To determine whether the influence of partisanship varies across these four conditions, we include a set of three dummy variables representing three categories and leaving the no partisan information/nonpar-

TABLE 3.2 Probit model of vote choice in experiment 2

VARIABLE	COEFFICIENT (STANDARD ERROR)
Party ID	0.062 (0.230)
Subtle partisan information/Partisan election	1.122 (0.620)
Subtle partisan information/Partisan election × Party ID	1.913* (0.678)
Subtle partisan information/Nonpartisan election	0.432 (0.305)
Subtle partisan information/Nonpartisan election × Party ID	0.174 (0.331)
No partisan information/Partisan election	−0.298 (0.361)
No partisan information/Partisan election × Party ID	1.235* (0.376)
Constant	−0.241 (0.213)
χ^2	58.89 ($p < 0.001$)
McKelvey/Zavoina r^2	0.518
% Correctly Predicted	73.1%
PRE	0.324
n	171

Notes: * denotes $p < 0.05$

tisan condition as the baseline category. We then also include the interaction of party identification with each of the three treatment categories. Results of the model appear in table 3.2.

Determining the effect of party identification under the different treatment conditions is not entirely straightforward, so we graphically present the effect of partisanship across the four treatment conditions in figure 3.1. Specifically, we present the discrete change in the predicted probability of voting for the Democratic candidate associated with a shift in partisanship from Republican to Democrat (–1 to +1 on party ID). In the condition where there was no partisan issue information in the vignette, but candidates' party affiliations were explicitly revealed, partisanship exerts a great deal of influence on outcomes, with a shift from Republican to Democrat increasing the probability of a Democratic vote by 0.742. In the condition with no partisan issue content in the vignette but a nonpartisan election format, shifting from Republican to Democrat has no statistically significant effect on vote choice. This is to be expected as subjects received no cue that could reasonably be expected to allow subjects to bring their partisanship to bear on their vote choice.

FIGURE 3.1. Discrete changes in the probability of voting for the Democrat across four treatment conditions

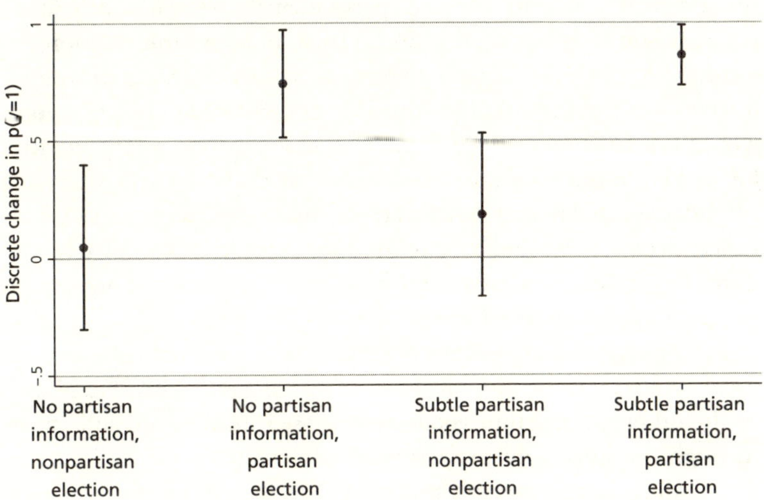

Note: Predicted probabilities based on the model in table 3.2.

In the condition with subtle partisan issue information and when partisan issue information was explicitly revealed, we again find strong effects of subject partisanship on vote choice (shifting from Republican to Democrat increases the probability of a Democratic vote by 0.86). However, in the nonpartisan version of the subtle partisan issue vignette, the partisanship has no statistically significant effect. To be sure, given the small sample size relative to the number of prompts, it may be that the effect of partisanship is simply too small to be detected with the sample size available in experiment 2. Even so, the results suggest that any effect that might be detected in a larger-scale experiment would be modest.

Discussion

The results of experiment 1 show that in a tightly controlled setting where candidate issue information gives voters cues about candidate partisanship, a nonpartisan election format will do little to mitigate the influence of partisanship on vote choice. Indeed, when the information voters have about candidates is abundant and reveals information about candidates' issue positions, there is no statistically significant difference in rates of partisan voting between the partisan and nonpartisan conditions. However, experiment 2 shows that when information about candidates' issue positions is limited (or completely absent), subjects' party identification has little or no influence on their voting decisions. Thus, in a low-information environment, the data suggest that nonpartisan elections can be effective at removing partisanship. It is unclear what criteria a voter would use in this condition; the fact that a voter cannot identify his or her co-partisan does not mean that the voter will select the candidate with the best qualifications, most experience, and so on. Indeed, vote choice under these conditions could be completely random. Regardless, we have identified conditions where nonpartisan elections appear to be effective.

However, given the results from our observational data, experiment 1 appears to be more realistic of actual campaigns. Despite all of the other information voters are exposed to, they are able to sift through the noise and properly identify the partisan affiliation of the candidates. It is possible that some elections in some states more closely resemble the conditions we created in experiment 2. If this is the case, then we would expect that voters would not make decisions based on the partisanship of the candidates. As state supreme court races become increasingly contested, competitive, and costly, we suspect that if the conditions in experiment 2 accurately characterize some current races, this is likely to be short-lived.

Conclusion

In chapter 2, our examination of observational data established that there are high rates of partisan voting even in nonpartisan elections. Our use of experiments to probe this finding further in this chapter not only confirms the possibility of highly partisan voting in nonpartisan elections but also allows us to explain an important reason why partisan voting is possible in nonpartisan elections. Specifically, when issue-oriented information about candidates is available, the explicit use of partisan labels is unnecessary to facilitate partisan voting. In conjunction with the findings from chapter 2, these results suggest that significant levels of issue information that gives voters cues about the partisanship of candidates must circulate in actual nonpartisan judicial elections. This information makes it possible for voters to cast ballots on the basis of their partisanship even in the absence of explicit partisan cues on the ballot.

This is not terribly surprising given the increase in competitiveness and contentiousness of state supreme court elections over the past couple of decades. While the *White* case (discussed in the introduction) formally removed any prohibitions on candidates taking positions on legal issues, scholars have shown it had no significant effect (Bonneau, Hall, and Streb 2011) on the conduct of elections in that candidates were signaling their party and ideology to voters long before 2002.

In terms of normative implications, given the electoral and legal environment, there may simply be no way to make nonpartisan elections "work." Indeed, even if somehow it were legally permissible to prohibit candidates from making statements that reveal their partisan affiliation, this would be a draconian constraint on the free speech of candidates. If a system requires such an imposition on freedom of speech, proponents of such a system have to make a compelling argument that the resulting benefits are worth the imposed costs.

In chapter 4, we turn our attention to another ballot cue utilized in some states: incumbency. Are incumbents better advantaged in states where voters are told which candidate is the current officeholder? And does this have different effects in partisan elections versus nonpartisan elections?

4

DOES ONE GOOD TERM DESERVE ANOTHER? INCUMBENCY AND VOTE CHOICE

Because most Ohioans have little contact with the judicial system, they know little about which judges do a good job and which do not. Candidates who can call themselves "judge" or "justice" have a significant advantage over even better-qualified opponents.
—*Toledo Blade,* "Editorial: Packing the Court"

One of the enduring findings in electoral politics is that incumbents generally fare better than non-incumbents. While this finding is reasonably well established, a veritable plethora of explanations exists for this incumbency advantage. Incumbents often enjoy greater name recognition than non-incumbents (Jacobson 2013). Some incumbents enjoy perquisites of office that bestow an electoral advantage (Cover and Brumberg 1982; Fiorina 1977; Shepsle 1978). Incumbents generally also enjoy the benefits of an established fund-raising network, a campaign staff with a demonstrated track record of success, and a set of constituents who have already voted to support them at least once before (Green and Krasno 1988).

Beyond these built-in advantages, incumbents often base their campaigns on messages that claim their experience. This is particularly true in judicial elections, where candidates have historically expressed themes of qualifications and experience. If voters indeed have some general preference to choose an incumbent over a non-incumbent (all else being equal), then judicial incumbents should have a formidable advantage over their opponents. Further, in some states, incumbent candidates are formally identified as such on the ballot, signaling to voters who might otherwise be undecided or uninformed about the candidates that they are individuals who have been carrying out the duties of the office.

In this chapter, we evaluate whether formal ballot information regarding incumbency affords incumbents an additional advantage in contestable judicial elections. Incumbency in judicial elections is not as straightforward as it is in other institutional settings. In addition to the fact that some judges are elected in partisan elections while others are elected in nonpartisan elections, not all judges come by their incumbency the same way. Some judges have previously won election to their seat (traditional incumbents), while about one-third of state supreme court judges were initially appointed to their position to fill a vacancy and so are running in an election for the first time (Bonneau and Hall 2009). While these judges are incumbents, they may not accrue all of the advantages of traditional incumbents (name recognition, established funding network, etc.). Using experimental research techniques, we take advantage of the ability to manipulate the presence or absence of a formal incumbency indicator on a vote choice question that mimics a ballot setting. If voters indeed have a preference for incumbents, all else being equal, we expect to see subjects who received a ballot cue regarding incumbency to be proportionally more supportive of the incumbent candidate over non-incumbents than subjects who received no such cue. Additionally, we examine whether the incumbency advantage varies based on (1) type of election and (2) type of incumbent.

The Incumbency Advantage

The existence of an incumbency advantage in congressional elections is taken as a given. Since 1980, the percentage of U.S. House incumbents seeking reelection who win has dropped below 90% in only three elections (1992, 2010, and 2012); never in that time period did the percentage drop below 85% (Ornstein et al. 2013). To be sure, highly vulnerable candidates, including those plagued by scandal or saddled with unpopular voting records, will often opt to retire rather than face a bruising election with an uncertain outcome. However, given the relatively modest number of retirements per election cycle, one can conclude with reasonable certainty that incumbents enjoy a considerable advantage over their challengers.

There are a variety of explanations for the favorable electoral fortunes of incumbents. Incumbents enjoy a measure of publicity just from conducting the business of their elective office, interacting with constituents, appearing in the news media in a variety of formats, and accepting speaking and other public engagements often offered to public servants. Jacobson (2013) notes that as a consequence of such publicity, candidates enjoy a formidable advantage in name recognition over their opponents. Fowler (2008) notes that high-profile appearances in the media can lead to substantial gains in campaign contributions as well.

Beyond general publicity, Cover and Brumberg (1982) note that candidates may use the perquisites of office to cultivate their constituents. In a randomized experiment, they demonstrate that receipt of a pamphlet from their congressperson boosted subjects' attitudes toward their congressperson relative to a control group who received no mailing. These attitudes persisted for months after receipt of the mailing.

Along similar lines, Fiorina (1977) argues that members of Congress in particular use their unique positions to provide information and services to their constituents. The ability to provide constituents with flags (particularly flags that have been flown over the Capitol), special guided tours, and assistance in navigating the federal bureaucracy enables members of Congress to credibly claim credit for helping constituents (Mayhew 1974). Indeed, casework may even have "ripple effects" where individuals may form a more favorable impression of an elected official on the basis of a positive casework experience of a friend, family member, or other acquaintance.

Cox and Katz (1996) argue that the advantages held by incumbents are multiplied because many high-quality challengers opt not to enter the race because of the diminished odds of victory against an entrenched incumbent and the potential harm a lost election may have on their reputations and political careers.

Beyond these postulates, an additional explanation may exist for the incumbency advantage: incumbency itself. Voters may have preferences for experienced candidates who have already been carrying out the obligations of the office. Shepsle (1978) makes a variant of this argument, claiming that more senior members of Congress are better positioned to bring distributive benefits to the home district.

The legislative literature is clear that, regardless of the precise source of the incumbency advantage, incumbents are advantaged when they run for reelection.

Incumbency and Judicial Elections

While the advantages of incumbency are considerable for many candidates, there are significant differences between judicial candidates and candidates for most other elective offices. While children are taught from a young age to write to their congressperson, we know of no comparable program inculcating a norm of writing or calling judges to promote specific policy agendas. It is also true that judges do not enjoy the same perquisites of office that are enjoyed by many other elected officials. A judge cannot send free mailings to his or her constituents trumpeting recent decisions the judge made, nor can a judge call a press conference to call attention to a pressing issue and inform his or her constituents how the judge plans to deal with the issue. However, incumbent judges can campaign as incumbents: they can say "Reelect Judge X" in their campaign commercials, and they can talk about their experience and record on the bench. Additionally, to the extent that they have previously won a race to attain their position, they have experience running a campaign and likely have an established financial network. Indeed, Baum (2003, 38–39; see also Bonneau and Cann 2011; Bonneau and Hall 2009) writes that in state supreme court elections, incumbents "usually enjoy at least a mild advantage over their opponents in name recognition prior to the campaign, and they can usually spend more money than their opponents to extend that advantage during the campaign." So, incumbent judges do share some, but certainly not all, of the same advantages as incumbent legislators.

At the aggregate level, scholars have found evidence of an incumbency advantage for judges. Bonneau and Hall (2009) find that the average percentage of the vote received by incumbents in contested state supreme court elections is 55.7% in partisan states and 57.9% in nonpartisan states. Additionally, between 1990 and 2004, only 5.2% of incumbents in nonpartisan states were defeated, while 30.0% of incumbents in partisan states lost their bids to keep their jobs.[1] To be sure, this 30% defeat rate is quite high in comparison to reelection rates for legislatures and executives; however, the vast majority of incumbents in partisan states are reelected.

There are three major institutional differences between judicial elections and elections to other offices. As mentioned above, some judges are elected in partisan elections while others are elected in nonpartisan elections. To date, studies of the incumbency advantage have been conducted on partisan races only. This is problematic because scholars have found that the partisan cue is among the most influential predictors of vote choice (A. Campbell et al. 1960). Thus, it may be the case that current studies understate the true incumbency advantage since it is mitigated by the partisan nature of the election. In the absence of party cues, incumbents may have a larger advantage than they do when party cues are present. This is an important point because scholars have found that three-fourths of municipal elections in the United States are nonpartisan (DeSantis and Renner 1991), and over half of all U.S. elections do not contain the party identifications of the candidates on the ballot (Adrian 1959).

A second major difference is that while almost every legislative incumbent has previously won election, approximately one-third of state supreme court incumbents are making their first run for office. This is because justices regularly retire before the end of their terms, and governors are empowered to fill the vacancy until the next scheduled election. Consequently, these appointed incumbents may not accrue all of the advantages of elected incumbents. To the extent that one source of the incumbency advantage is that incumbents have previously run a statewide campaign and have an established network of campaign donors, these factors are absent for appointed incumbents. Looking at aggregate data, Bonneau (2005, 835) found that "an incumbent who has been appointed to the bench has more electoral advantages than her nonincumbent challenger. However, she does not benefit as much from her incumbency as her colleagues who have faced the electorate before." Bonneau and Hall (2009) find that appointed incumbents perform about 3.3% worse than elected incumbents, other things being equal. This suggests that voters may respond differently to different types of incumbents.

A third, and final, difference is the presence of the "incumbent" designation on the ballot. In six states (Arkansas, Georgia, Idaho,

Michigan, Minnesota, and Oregon), the incumbent is explicitly designated as such on the ballot. Thus, voters know which candidate is the incumbent. Unfortunately, all of these states utilize nonpartisan elections so we cannot determine whether incumbency can mitigate the effects of partisanship using observational data. However, we can do this using experimental data where we can provide subjects with both the partisan affiliation of the candidate and denote incumbency.

Hypotheses

We seek to test the specific possibility that voters have a preference for supporting an incumbent aside from the structural advantages of incumbency. The blanket hypothesis is simple, holding that voters prefer an individual who has previously held an office to someone who lacks such experience. While some of the rationale supporting this hypothesis for congressional elections may not apply in judicial elections (specifically the notion that senior incumbents are better positioned to channel distributive benefits to their constituents), other aspects of the rationale, especially the focus on qualifications and experience, are arguably facets of electoral politics that are more salient in judicial elections.

We seek to operationalize this hypothesis in a particular manner. Several states specifically indicate on the ballot which candidates (if any) are incumbents.[2] If voters have a specific preference for incumbents, all else being equal, we would expect that an explicit indicator of incumbency on the ballot would advantage the incumbent independently of any structural advantage that may apply in varying degrees to different candidates. Klein and Baum (2001) proposed a similar experiment, but their study differs in a number of important respects. First, rather than offering a tightly controlled description of the candidates to be given to subjects, they relied on the citizens' exposure to actual campaigns, which could result in dramatic variance across subjects in what they know about the candidates. In our experiment, we present all subjects with carefully controlled information about the candidates. Second, Klein and Baum are not looking at the effects of ballot cues on vote choice, since the candidates' occupations, residency, and party identification are not provided on the ballot to voters in Ohio. Regardless of the group to which group the respondents were randomly assigned, they all experienced the *same* ballot when they went to vote. In our study, our subjects are exposed to varying cues. Third, Klein and Baum list both candidates' current occupation rather than specifically denoting which candidate was the incumbent. Finally, because Klein and Baum used existing candidates, they were unable to use experimental manipulations of potential mediating and moderating variables in a rigorous way. While they varied indicators of partisanship, they could not determine whether the voters had or had not encountered the party identifications of the candidates in the course of the election. Our experimental manipulations allow us to systematically vary whether partisan information is released about the candidates in a formal way. This is important because such manipulations enable us to rigorously evaluate whether ballot information regarding candidates affects voters differently in the absence of partisan cues than in their presence. Additionally, our design allows us to systematically manipulate whether the incumbent was elected previously (which may benefit the incumbent more) or appointed to serve until the next election. Our formal hypotheses are, then:

H4.1: Subjects will be more likely to vote for a particular judicial candidate if they are in a treatment group that receives a formal indication of the candidate's incumbency status than if they are in a treatment group where incumbency status is not indicated on the ballot.

H4.2: The effect of a formal ballot indicator of incumbency on judicial vote choice will be larger in nonpartisan elections than in partisan elections.

H4.3: The effect of a formal ballot indicator of incumbency on judicial vote choice will be larger for elected incumbents than for appointed incumbents.

Experimental Design

To evaluate the effect of ballot information about incumbency, we devised a simple experiment. We created a fully crossed 2×2×2 experimental design (for a total of eight distinct treatment conditions) to evaluate whether the effect of ballot information is conditional on the election format (partisan versus nonpartisan) and whether the incumbent ascended to office by election or appointment.

We devised a simple vignette describing two hypothetical candidates running for election to their state supreme court. The vignettes pit two candidates against each other and offer basic descriptions of the candidates' backgrounds, education, and experience. The vignettes are held constant with the exception of simple manipulations that indicate whether the election was partisan or not (indicating the party identification of the candidates in the partisan case) and whether the incumbent in the race was elected to office or appointed to fill out a term. The vignette was followed by a vote choice question, which included the names of the candidates, their party affiliation (if the vignette was for a partisan election), and the word "incumbent" beside the name (if the individual was assigned to a treatment condition that listed incumbency on the ballot). The text of the vignettes and the wording of the vote choice question can be found in appendix C. The result is eight distinct treatments (partisan, elected, incumbency on the ballot; partisan, elected, no incumbency on the ballot; nonpartisan, elected, incumbency on the ballot; nonpartisan, elected, no incumbency on the ballot; partisan, appointed, incumbency on the ballot; partisan, appointed, no incumbency on the ballot; nonpartisan, appointed, incumbency on the ballot; and nonpartisan, appointed, no incumbency on the ballot). Subjects were randomly assigned with an equal probability to each treatment.

Subjects were recruited in two waves in February and March 2013. The first wave was drawn from Amazon's Mechanical Turk (mTurk) service and was administered to subjects online, and the second was drawn from undergraduate students at a western university who completed the same survey on paper.[3] While both are convenience samples, which may diminish the external validity of the results, they are two very different convenience samples, with the mTurk sample being somewhat more liberal than the U.S. population and the university sample being somewhat more conservative. Moreover, the study affords the tightly controlled internal validity that only a carefully controlled experiment can provide.

Given that any experimental subject (whether on mTurk or otherwise) may fail to make thoughtful responses to questions, we followed the best practice of embedding a simple comprehension question in our mTurk sample to ensure the subject was paying attention and understanding the study (consider Horton, Rand, and Zeckhauser 2011). In our instance, subjects read a passage about a congressional election and were then asked which candidate was the Democrat in the surveys. Subjects who failed to correctly answer this question were excluded from the core analysis because they were not spending sufficient time to complete the exercise. After removing subjects who did not correctly answer the comprehension question, we have a total of 489 respondents (377 from mTurk and 112 from the university student sample) spread approximately equally across experimental conditions. Simple comparisons of respondents' expressed vote choices can then be made to determine the effect of ballot indicators of incumbency under different treatment conditions.

Results

We begin our presentation of results with a simple test of the overall hypothesis that formal identification of the incumbent on the ballot affects vote choice. Because the design is fully crossed, any effects of partisan/nonpartisan election format are mitigated in looking for the overall effect of listing incumbency on the ballot. Table 4.1 shows subjects' expressed vote choices by whether or not they received a treatment that indicated incumbency as part of the vote choice question.

Surprisingly, the overall analysis finds no statistically significant effect of the incumbency indicator on vote choice. The sample percentages voting for the incumbent differ by a mere 1.6%. On the basis of this, we would conclude that the incumbency advantage in judicial elections is not derived from having incumbency denoted on the ballot. Voters are not responsive to the incumbency cue. While scholars have found an incumbency advantage at the aggregate level (Bonneau and Cann 2011; Bonneau and Hall 2009), it does not appear that the source of this advantage is in ballot cues.

However, our hypotheses posit that effect sizes may be larger in treatment conditions with nonpartisan elections where voters receive no explicit partisan cues on the ballot and with elected incumbents who may benefit more from voters who may give greater credit to incumbents who have served a longer period of time.

Table 4.2 shows the effect of including incumbency in both partisan and nonpartisan election formats. In treatments that included

TABLE 4.1 Vote choice by incumbency indication

	INCUMBENCY NOT INDICATED (%)	INCUMBENCY INDICATED (%)	TOTAL (%)
Voted for incumbent	121 (51.9)	137 (53.5)	258 (52.8)
Voted for non-incumbent	92 (39.5)	95 (37.1)	187 (38.2)
Indicated abstention	20 (8.6)	24 (9.4)	44 (9.0)
Total	233	256	489

Note: $\chi^2 = 0.323$, $p = 0.851$; difference of proportions on "voted for the incumbent" cells $p = 0.799$.

TABLE 4.2 Vote choice by incumbency indication and election format

	PARTISAN FORMAT		NONPARTISAN FORMAT	
	INCUMBENCY NOT INDICATED (%)	INCUMBENCY INDICATED (%)	INCUMBENCY NOT INDICATED (%)	INCUMBENCY INDICATED (%)
Voted for incumbent	66 (57.9)	67 (51.5)	55 (46.2)	70 (56.0)
Voted for non-incumbent	37 (32.5)	51 (38.9)	55 (46.2)	44 (35.2)
Indicated abstention	11 (9.7)	13 (9.9)	9 (7.6)	11 (8.8)
Total	114	131	119	125

Note: For partisan elections: $\chi^2 = 1.228$, $p = 0.541$; difference of proportions on "voted for the incumbent" cells $p = 0.435$. For nonpartisan elections: $\chi^2 = 3.0765$, $p = 0.251$; difference of proportions on "voted for the incumbent" cells $p = 0.277$.

a partisan election, an incumbency indicator on the vote choice question slightly decreased support for the incumbent, while in the nonpartisan condition there was a modest increase in support for the incumbent when he was identified as such in the vote choice question. However, neither of these effects is statistically significant at conventional levels using either a chi-square test or a difference of proportions *z*-test on the proportion of subjects supporting the incumbent.

TABLE 4.3 Vote choice by incumbency indication and elected versus appointed incumbency status

	ELECTED INCUMBENT		APPOINTED INCUMBENT	
	INCUMBENCY NOT INDICATED (%)	INCUMBENCY INDICATED (%)	INCUMBENCY NOT INDICATED (%)	INCUMBENCY INDICATED (%)
Voted for incumbent	61 (49.6)	69 (55.2)	60 (54.6)	68 (51.9)
Voted for non-incumbent	48 (39.0)	42 (33.6)	44 (40.0)	53 (40.5)
Indicated abstention	14 (11.3)	14 (11.2)	6 (5.5)	10 (7.6)
Total	123	125	110	131

Note: For elected incumbents, $\chi^2 = 0.876$, $p = 0.645$; difference of proportions on "voted for the incumbent" cells $p = 0.522$. For appointed incumbents, $\chi^2 = 0.509$, $p = 0.775$; difference of proportions on "voted for the incumbent" cells $p = 0.765$.

In table 4.3, we partition the data in a different manner, arraying the effects of a ballot incumbency indicator on vote choice in treatments where we varied whether the incumbent was elected or appointed. Again, there is little substantive difference between the two, with only a slight increase in vote total for an elected incumbent when incumbency is indicated on the ballot and a slight decrease in vote total for an appointed incumbent when incumbency is specifically indicated on the vote choice question. None of these effects are statistically significant.

Finally, we take advantage of the fully crossed structure of the data to determine whether the effect of formal indication of incumbency on the ballot varies more when there are partisan elections and elected incumbents, partisan elections and appointed incumbents, nonpartisan elections and elected incumbents, and nonpartisan elections and appointed incumbents. While the sample sizes become small when the data are parsed this finely, the results, presented in tables 4.4 and 4.5, are consistent with earlier results.[4]

When comparing vote choice for the incumbent in our vignettes on situations with and without a formal incumbency indicator on

TABLE 4.4 Vote choice by incumbency indication and elected versus appointed incumbency status for partisan elections

	ELECTED INCUMBENT		APPOINTED INCUMBENT	
	INCUMBENCY NOT INDICATED (%)	INCUMBENCY INDICATED (%)	INCUMBENCY NOT INDICATED (%)	INCUMBENCY INDICATED (%)
Voted for incumbent	34 (54.8)	34 (54.8)	32 (61.5)	33 (47.8)
Voted for non-incumbent	18 (29.0)	20 (32.3)	19 (36.5)	31 (44.9)
Indicated abstention	10 (16.1)	8 (12.9)	1 (1.9)	5 (7.3)
Total	62	62	52	69

Note: For elected incumbents: $\chi^2 = 0.876$, $p = 0.645$; difference of proportions on "voted for the incumbent" cells p=0.522. For appointed incumbents: $\chi^2 = 0.509$, $p = 0.775$; difference of proportions on "voted for the incumbent" cells $p = 0.765$.

TABLE 4.5 Vote choice by incumbency indication and elected versus appointed incumbency status for nonpartisan elections

	ELECTED INCUMBENT		APPOINTED INCUMBENT	
	INCUMBENCY NOT INDICATED (%)	INCUMBENCY INDICATED (%)	INCUMBENCY NOT INDICATED (%)	INCUMBENCY INDICATED (%)
Voted for incumbent	27 (44.3)	35 (55.6)	28 (48.3)	35 (56.5)
Voted for non-incumbent	30 (49.2)	22 (34.9)	25 (43.1)	22 (35.5)
Indicated abstention	4 (6.6)	6 (9.5)	5 (8.6)	5 (8.1)
Total	61	63	58	62

Note: For elected incumbents: $\chi^2 = 2.632$, $p = 0.268$; difference of proportions on "voted for the incumbent" cells $p = 0.378$. For appointed incumbents: $\chi^2 = 0.837$, $p = 0.658$; difference of proportions on "voted for the incumbent" cells $p = 0.519$.

the vote choice question in the four specific settings derived from crossing partisan versus nonpartisan format and elected versus appointed incumbents, we find no statistically significant effects.

In sum, the results show that there is no difference in vote totals based on the provision of incumbency on the ballot. Unlike our results for partisanship, in this case ballot cues do not affect the performance of candidates.

Validation with Observational Data

While the experimental results are clear, we feel the ideal combination of evidence is support from both experimental and observational data that can confirm a result with both high internal validity experiments and high external validity observational data. As such, we take a moment here to assess whether there is any observable difference in the incumbency advantage in judicial elections between states where incumbency is listed on the ballot and states where it is not. While previous studies have examined this question at the aggregate level (e.g., Bonneau and Hall 2009), none have looked at the effects of ballot cues.

We can most readily conduct this test by comparing the vote share incumbents receive in states where incumbency appears on the ballot with the vote share incumbents receive in states where incumbency does not appear on the ballot.[5] To make such a comparison, we estimate an OLS regression model with the percentage of the vote received by the incumbent as the dependent variable and a dichotomous indicator for whether the race took place in a state that indicates incumbency on the ballot as the primary independent variable of interest. We also include standard control variables from the literature on state high court elections (e.g., Bonneau and Hall 2009). Specifically, we include an indicator for whether an election is partisan (versus nonpartisan) in election format because of the possibility that incumbency could be used as a signal to replace partisanship in the absence of partisan cues. We control for challenger quality to account for the lower vote totals incumbents will likely receive when facing stronger opponents. Challenger quality is defined as whether the challenger in the race has previously served as a judge (Hall and Bonneau 2008). We include campaign spending (in logged 1990 dollars) for both the incumbent and the challenger;

TABLE 4.6 OLS regression model of incumbent vote share

	COEFFICIENT (STANDARD ERROR)
Incumbency on the ballot	−0.914 (2.299)
Partisan format	−2.322 (1.927)
Quality challenger	−2.984 (1.881)
ln(incumbent spending)	1.274* (0.646)
ln(challenger spending)	−1.725* (0.505)
Folded MPI	3.723 (10.536)
District (vs. statewide) election	−1.778 (2.119)
Multimember (vs. single-member) district	6.396* (3.054)
Constant	56.143* (6.127)
R^2	0.403
RMSE	8.497
n	166

Note: *$p < 0.05$, one-tailed.

campaign spending is logged to account for diminishing returns to campaign spending in judicial elections (Bonneau and Cann 2011). We include Ceasar and Saldin's (2005) major party index (folded around 0.5) to control for the general competitiveness of the state political environment. Finally, we include two dichotomous indicators for the district structure: district-based versus statewide elections and multimember versus single-member districts.

We run this model on data from the 166 contested state supreme court elections (from all states holding contestable judicial elections) between 1990 and 2004 that involved an incumbent.[6] Standard errors for the model are clustered by state. Results of the model appear in table 4.6.

The coefficient on the variable for whether incumbency is listed on the ballot is negative, suggesting that if anything, the indicator of incumbency *decreases* incumbent vote share, though the effect is far from statistically significant. Rather than being helped directly by incumbency, incumbents seem to be most helped by spending more money on their campaigns (and by their opponents spending less). The lack of significance of the formal incumbency indicator should not be taken to mean that incumbents do not enjoy an advantage in state supreme court elections; rather it simply tells us that the advantage does not come from being specifically identified as such (e.g. citizens' general preference for incumbents over non-incumbents). Instead, the incumbency advantage springs from the ability to raise more funds, better name recognition, and other such factors (e.g., Jacobson 2013).[7]

Conclusion

While it is well documented that judicial incumbents enjoy a host of advantages in elections (Bonneau 2005; Bonneau and Hall 2009), the results we present here suggest that being presented on the ballot as the incumbent is not among them. In our experiments, voters demonstrated no clear preference for the incumbent regardless of election format or the elected versus appointed status of the judge. This was confirmed in our observational data analysis. While surprising, our results for judicial elections square with the findings of Brown (2013), who found that in similar experimental manipulations involving congressional candidates varying the presence of an incumbent (and the incumbent's length of tenure) and the presence of party labels had no effect on voters' preferences between candidates. They are also consistent with the findings of Ansolabehere and Pettigrew's (2013) manipulation of the length of tenure in Congress on citizens' preferences for hypothetical candidates described in experimental vignettes. The results also square with the findings of Klein and Baum (2001), who had listed candidates by occupation rather than by a formal indicator of incumbency on a simulated ballot.

This is not to say that incumbency is unimportant. A host of structural advantages in terms of running an effective campaign, a developed fund-raising network, name recognition, and more combine to give incumbents a formidable electoral advantage. Our results do suggest, however, that voters do not presume that all else being equal, an incumbent is a better candidate than a non-incumbent. The combination of experimental and observational evidence makes us quite confident in this conclusion.

This finding has interesting normative implications for candidates seeking judicial office. If incumbency in itself were the source of the formidable incumbency advantage, there would be little a judicial candidate could do. However, given that the structural advantages of judicial incumbency seem to stem instead from factors such as name recognition and fund-raising, it seems that a quality challenger with a strong reputation and fund-raising aptitude would be able to compete even in the face of the incumbency advantage (Bonneau and Hall 2009; Hall and Bonneau 2006).

In terms of the debate over judicial selection, the findings here suggest that providing information (other than the party identification of the candidates) on the ballot will not unduly influence voters. Thus, those concerned about the basis by which voters make their decisions should focus their efforts on other things besides the ballot. At the same time, those who are worried that the state is unfairly advantaging incumbents by informing voters which candidate is the incumbent can rest easy: no such advantage is accruing to incumbents.

Thus far, we have focused our attention exclusively on competitive elections (i.e., elections with more than one candidate). However, a plurality of state supreme court justices retain their jobs in uncontested retention elections. In chapter 5, we turn our attention to these races to examine what factors voters consider when they make the decision to keep (or not keep) an incumbent judge.

5

VOTING YES: RETENTION ELECTIONS

States should look to reforms that take political pressure out of the judicial selection process. In recent years, I have advocated the system used in my home state of Arizona, where a bipartisan nominating committee recommends a pool of qualified candidates from which the governor appoints judges to fill vacancies. Voters then hold judges accountable in retention elections.

—Sandra Day O'Connor, April 2013 interview with Justice at Stake

Thus far, we have confined our analysis to contestable state supreme court elections; that is, those elections that are capable of involving more than one candidate. These elections mirror those for executives and legislatures throughout the United States. However, a sizable minority of state supreme court elections are not contestable; voters are able to vote to keep (or not keep) the incumbent, but they are not given an alternative candidate for whom to vote. These elections are referred to as retention elections, and they are commonly a component of the so-called merit selection system. We discussed how these elections generally operate in the introduction, with candidates initially being appointed to the bench by the governor from a list generated by a selection committee and candidates keeping their jobs in periodic retention elections.[1] The key distinguishing feature between these elections and the ones discussed in previous chapters is that there is not the possibility for electoral competition.

With some notable exceptions discussed below, we understand very little about how citizens decide to vote in these elections. Even more so than other state supreme court elections, retention elections are very low-information affairs. Historically, retention candidates only rarely put up campaign signs, distribute materials, run ads, or spend any money at all on their retention bids, with campaign spending on retention elections making up only 1% of the total expenditures on all judicial elections (partisan, quasi-partisan, nonpartisan, and retention) nationally in the 2000–2009 time period (Skaggs et al. 2011). As such, what information do voters have to go on in such a low-information environment?

In this chapter, we explore the determinants of vote choice in retention elections. Consistent with past research and contrary to the language of pro-retention election advocates, we find that these races are governed by the tendency of voters to simply vote "yes." This default "yes" position undermines the argument that retention elections effectively promote accountability. Interestingly, these elections do not remove partisan voting. Despite the predisposition of voters to retain judges, Democratic voters are significantly more likely to vote to keep judges appointed by Democratic governors, and Republican voters are significantly more likely to vote to retain judges appointed by Republican governors. Even in state supreme court retention elections, the effects of partisan voting can be found. On the positive side, voter participation in retention elections is higher than participation in nonpartisan races, though it falls far short of the rates of participation found in partisan elections.

Retention Elections: What We Know and What We Don't Know

Much of what we know about retention elections comes from Larry Aspin, who collects data on them every two years and then publishes an article documenting recent trends. Currently, Aspin's (2011) work spans from 1964 to 2010 (though Aspin has done some work, thus far unpublished, on the 2012 elections, which we discuss below) and involves retention elections at all levels of the judiciary, not just state supreme courts. This excellent work, along with research from other scholars, reveals several interesting features of judicial elections. First, according to Aspin (2011) the average percentage of the vote in 2010 was 69.5%. This seems quite high in the context of competitive elections; however, this was the lowest average since 1964. That is, since 1964, candidates standing for retention have earned at least 70% of the affirmative vote. In 2012, the percentage jumped to 73.7% (Aspin 2013). Looking only at state supreme court elections from 1990 to 2004, Bonneau and Hall (2009) find that the average percentage of the vote is 71.0%, and Hall (2001) found that from 1980 to 1994 only 2.6% were won with less than 55% of the vote. Interestingly, Olson (2001) finds that judges receiving low performance evaluation scores do not receive lower vote totals, though an organized opposition campaign does lead to a small decrease in vote totals, calling into question the effectiveness of providing information about judicial performance to the voters.

Second, according to Aspin (2011), the lowest percentage of the affirmative vote in 2010 came from Alaska and Iowa (63.4%) followed closely by Oklahoma (63.5%). The highest was Maryland (85.4%), Utah (77.3%), and Illinois (75.8%). Even in states at the bottom of the list, incumbents receive the vast majority of the votes. Related to this is the issue of defeats. Fitzpatrick (2009) reports that incumbents are returned to office 99% of the time across the United States. Bonneau and Hall (2009) report that the defeat rate for incumbents in retention elections from 1990 to 2004 was 1.3%. This is consistent with what one would expect given the high percentage of the affirmative vote received by incumbents.

Third, ballot roll-off in 2010 ranged from 18.6% (Alaska) to 42.9% (Arizona). These numbers are conservative when one takes into account that voter participation was 4% higher in 2010 than 2008, and ballot roll-off in 2010 was the lowest it has been in forty years.[2] Ballot roll-off figures are often higher in retention elections than in contestable elections. Interestingly, Arizona, the state that former justice Sandra Day O'Connor has lauded as a model system (Justice 2013), has the lowest level of voter participation across all retention states in 2008, 2010, and 2012. Focusing only on state supreme courts, Bonneau and Hall (2009) found that average roll-off in retention elections is 25.7% from 1990 to 2004, which is a dramatic improvement in participation from the roll-off figures of 36%–40% (depending on if the election was held in a presidential year or not) reported by Dubois (1979, table 1).

Fourth, Hall (2001) examined the factors that determine the percentage of affirmative votes earned by candidates. She found that while candidate-based factors did not seem to affect the vote total, "supreme court justices who stand for retention in states characterized by competitive party politics or in elections with partisan cross-pressures (measured with reference to gubernatorial races) receive a significantly lower proportion of positive votes" (Hall 2001, 324). That is, judges standing for retention were not immune from political pressures, contrary to the arguments made by advocates of retention elections. Savchak and Barghothi (2007, 404), examining decisions made by state supreme court justices from 1995 to 1997, find something similar: "judges become more concerned with, and responsive to, citizens when they are about to be evaluated by the public in the retention election."

The biggest gap in our knowledge about retention elections has to do with the determinants of participation and the affirmative vote. Simply put, we have no empirical data on the choices made by voters. In this chapter, we utilize the 2012 CCES survey to examine these choices. We ask all respondents (1) if they voted in the retention election and (2) if they voted yes. In states where there was more than one race on the ballot, we ask respondents these questions for only one randomly selected race. This will allow us to examine candidate- and race-specific factors and ascertain why voters participate in retention elections and why they choose to retain (or not retain) incumbents.

Participation in Retention Elections

Existing scholarship compares the level of ballot roll-off across states with different types of judicial retention systems (partisan, nonpartisan, and retention systems). Consistent with our own findings in chapter 1, these comparisons uniformly identify a higher level of participation in partisan elections than in nonpartisan elections (Bonneau and Hall 2009; Hall 2007). However, there are competing propositions for whether contestable nonpartisan elections fare better or worse than retention elections at promoting participation. On one hand, a contestable nonpartisan election affords voters a choice between candidates, which may make the prospect of voting seem more important. Moreover, as the candidates campaign against one another, they provide information that may make the voting decision easier for voters. Alternatively, though, the lack of partisan information on the ballot could lead some individuals who know little about the candidates to abstain from the election, feeling they cannot distinguish between the candidates well enough to warrant participation.[3] In a retention election, rather than having to choose between two candidates (where voters may lack information about which candidate is better), voters are simply asked whether to retain a sitting judge or not. A ballot question framed in this way simplifies the voting decision and suggests the application of a simple retrospective evaluation of how the voter feels about their state's justice system or the judge in particular. For many individuals who feel their state's justice system performs adequately, a default "yes" vote becomes the norm (though a smaller number of people who are consistently disgruntled may become default "no" voters). In the absence of a need to compare the one judge with another judge, many voters may simply vote "yes" and move on to the rest of the ballot.

MODELING PARTICIPATION

While the 2010 CCES asked no questions about participation in retention elections, the 2012 CCES asked about voter participation and vote choice not only for respondents in contestable election states but also for all respondents in states that held retention elections. As with the contestable election states, respondents in retention election states were randomly assigned to answer one vote choice question about one of the races in their state. A list of the races analyzed in this chapter can be found in appendix B.

Our goal is not to simply evaluate the predictors of participation in retention elections, but to compare rates of participation in retention elections with other formats. We begin our model formulation with the model we specified in chapter 1 assessing turnout in contestable judicial elections. We pool data from contestable election states with the data for verified turnout and ballot roll-off for respondents living in retention election states. We then estimate a Heckman probit model similar to the one used in chapter 1 where

TABLE 5.1 Heckman probit model of participation in contestable and retention elections, 2012 CCES

	ROLL-OFF	TURNOUT
Partisan election	−0.894* (0.068)	—
Quasi-partisan election	−0.607* (0.077)	—
Nonpartisan election	−0.290* (0.064)	—
College	−0.038 (0.039)	0.382* (0.042)
White	0.018 (0.051)	0.122* (0.051)
Male	−0.182* (0.039)	−0.025 (0.039)
Weekly church	0.027 (0.044)	0.246* (0.045)
Union membership	0.027 (0.059)	0.079 (0.066)
Homeowner	−0.046 (0.046)	0.350* (0.042)
Competitive environment	—	−0.002 (0.005)
Close gubernatorial race	—	0.086* (0.040)
Close senate race	—	0.158* (0.158)
Constant	−0.662* (0.057)	0.253* (0.070)
Wald χ^2	314.20 ($p < 0.001$)	
ρ	0.994 (0.006)	
Wald test of $\rho = 0$	906.99 ($p < 0.001$)	
n	16,941 (13879 uncensored/3062 censored)	

Note: *$p < 0.05$, two-tailed. Standard errors in parentheses.

we examined participation in contestable elections. Recognizing, as we did before, that individuals are drawn to the polls by up-ballot races, we model the probability of turnout in the first-stage equation as a function of education, race, gender, church attendance, union membership, home ownership, the state's general competitiveness (measured using the folded major-party index), and the presence of a close senatorial or gubernatorial race on the ballot. In the second equation we model the probability that a voter elects not to participate in a state supreme court election. We model roll-off using a similar set of variables as in chapter 1, using a set of indicators for

TABLE 5.2 Predicted probabilities of roll-off by election format

	PREDICTED PROBABILITY	STANDARD ERROR	95% CONFIDENCE INTERVAL
Partisan election	0.051	0.010	(0.032, 0.072)
Quasi-partisan election	0.092	0.010	(0.072, 0.112)
Nonpartisan election	0.162	0.017	(0.130, 0.195)
Retention election	0.254	0.027	(0.200, 0.307)

Note: Predicted probabilities are the probability of rolling-off conditional on having voted derived from the model in table 5.1.

election format (partisan, quasi-partisan, and nonpartisan with retention elections as the reference category), education, race, gender, church attendance, union membership, and home ownership.[4] The results of the model appear in table 5.1.

As the results for the turnout equation are similar to the results found in chapter 1, we focus here on the results from the roll-off equation. As we found in chapter 1, the most substantial influence on participation in judicial elections is the election format. Table 5.2 shows the predicted probabilities of roll-off holding the independent variables constant at their means (for continuous variables) or modal (for dichotomous variables) values.[5]

Partisan elections have the lowest level of roll-off compared to the other election formats with a predicted probability of roll-off at 0.051; quasi-partisan elections follow with a predicted probability of 0.092. Nonpartisan elections come in with the next highest level of roll-off at 0.162 and retention elections have the highest level of predicted roll-off, with just over one-fourth of voters of this profile being predicted to skip voting in a judicial election.

Among our individual-level control variables, men appear to be modestly less likely to roll-off than women. Several controls that showed significant effects in chapter 1, including education, church attendance, and home ownership, are not statistically significant at the conventional 0.05 level in this model. This suggests that while education and home ownership may help distinguish between those who roll-off and those who do not in contestable elections, the effect of these variables on roll-off in retention elections is minimal.

IMPLICATIONS

Studies that simply compare average levels of roll-off across different systems may misestimate the effect of election format on roll-off because they do not control for individual-level factors. Additionally, simple comparisons of mean roll-off rates do not account for the selection effects we address using the Heckman correction. Using appropriate statistical techniques, we confirm that low levels of ballot roll-off are a strength of the partisan election format. We find, however, this is a strength not shared by either contested nonpartisan elections or retention elections. While some have posited that the contested nature of nonpartisan elections alone would raise turnout, our results suggest otherwise. When one considers that our CCES results only include vote choice in contested nonpartisan and partisan elections (that is, elections involving two major-party candidates), it seems likely that if uncontested nonpartisan elections were included, the advantage of nonpartisan elections over retention elections would be relatively small.

Vote Choice in Judicial Retention Elections

Beyond just considering whether citizens choose to vote in retention elections, we seek to understand why citizens vote the way they do. It is at least as important to understand citizens' votes to retain or not retain a judge as it is to understand their decision to participate in an election. As such, we turn to the task of understanding the determinants of voting behavior in state high court retention elections.

Retention elections are promoted as an election format that provides many benefits similar to an appointment system (specifically in terms of isolation from political factors) while still engendering a measure of accountability to voters. Retention elections are nonpartisan—parties do not nominate candidates because only the incumbent can qualify for the ballot, and party affiliations are not listed on the ballot alongside the names of the candidate. Several concerns have been raised about the effectiveness of retention elections to promote accountability, in part because retention candidates seldom lose (Aspin 2011), and in part because the relationship between public opinion and judicial decisions is rather modest for judges who face retention elections (Cann and Wilhelm 2011).

In our evaluation of vote choice in judicial elections in this chapter, we evaluate the extent to which retention elections isolate judges from political factors. In particular, we wish to explore the extent to which partisanship influences voters' decisions in retention elections. In chapters 2 and 3, we argued that in nonpartisan elections, many voters are able to discern the partisanship of the candidates in nonpartisan elections. In retention elections, this task could perhaps be easier than in contestable nonpartisan elections because partisanship can be easily inferred from the party of the appointing governor.[6] However, in retention elections there is typically less issue information circulating because candidates rarely campaign (Skaggs et al. 2011). The lack of information circulating about the candidates may reduce the ability of voters to infer partisanship, leading voters to base their voting decisions on matters other than partisanship (such as retrospective evaluations of the court system or the judge). The influence of partisanship in retention elections is an empirical question that we are positioned to test for the first time because the 2012 CCES provides a basis on which we can observe the party identification of individual voters as well as their expressed vote choice in retention elections. Inferring party affiliations of judges from their appointed governors (or other means, if necessary, along the lines of the methods we employed to complete a similar task in chapter 2), we can determine whether Democrats (Republicans) are more likely to vote "yes" when the judicial candidate up for retention is a Democrat (Republican).

In the absence of partisanship, though, it is possible that candidates use incumbency (Schaffner, Streb, and Wright 2001), race (Pomper 1966), or gender (Squire and Smith 1988) as a basis on which to cast their votes. While nonpartisan elections may diminish the influence of partisanship in politics, if it is replaced with racial or gender-based voting, the outcome may be normatively less desirable than partisan voting. This is of particular concern given the racial- and gender-bias that has been found in Judicial Performance Evaluations, which are present in many states that utilize retention elections (Gill, Lazos, and Waters 2011). To determine the relative influence of these factors, we build a statistical model of the decision to vote "yes" in state high court retention elections.

MODELING VOTE CHOICE IN RETENTION ELECTIONS

As we described above, the 2012 CCES assigned respondents in retention election states at random to one of the state high court retention elections in their state.[7] These respondents were asked whether they participated in the retention election and, if they did, whether they voted to retain the candidate. A respondent's reported vote choice serves as our dependent variable (coded 1 = retain, 0 = do not retain) in a probit model of vote choice. As previously, we use only the reported vote choice of individuals who were verified to have actually voted.

To evaluate the effect of partisanship on vote choice in retention elections, we use a pair of dichotomous indicators for Republican and Democratic Party affiliation, leaving independents as the reference category. Naturally, the effect of being a Democrat or Republican on vote choice will be conditional on the party affiliation of the candidate facing retention. We make the effect of partisanship conditional on the party affiliation of the retention candidate[8] by including a dichotomous indicator for the candidate's party (1 = Democrat, 0 = Republican) and the interaction of the candidate's party with both the indicator for Republican and Democratic Party membership. This allows us to determine the effect of partisanship on the probability of a "yes" vote when the retention candidate is a Republican versus when the candidate is a Democrat.

Beyond partisanship, voters may lean on alternative cues about the candidate when deciding whether to retain him or her. In contestable nonpartisan elections, Schaffner, Streb, and Wright (2001) suggest that incumbents enjoy a more formidable advantage in the absence of partisan cues. Although all judges facing retention are incumbents, some of them are facing their first retention bid while others have actually stood before voters and have been retained previously. We include a dichotomous indicator for whether the retention candidate has previously prevailed in a retention election (1 = previously retained, 0 = first retention election).

Chief justices enjoy a measure of added visibility. In many instances they are selected by a vote of their peers; in others, they are retained in a specific "chief judge seat" by voters. The designation "chief judge" may even appear on the ballot. This designation may increase the likelihood of voters supporting chief judges' retention bids. Accordingly, we include a dichotomous indicator in the model for chief judges (1 = chief, 0 = associate).

While campaigning has traditionally been uncommon in retention elections, recent years have seen several campaigns waged by outside groups against judges facing retention. When such campaigns arise, retention candidates (or groups supporting them) often respond with campaign efforts of their own. In our sample of voters in twenty-nine retention races in the 2012 CCES, we observed five races in which organized campaigns formed to oppose the retention of judges. One was in Iowa, where sitting justice David Wiggins faced reprisal for a case legalizing same-sex marriage in Iowa (three of Wiggins's colleagues were defeated for retention in 2010 over the same decision). A second was in Arizona, where Justice John Pelander was opposed by Tea Party groups that were upset over Pelander's role in a ruling that would have allowed an election reform ballot initiative to move forward. The other three races were in Florida, where several conservative groups worked to deny retention to three Florida Supreme Court justices (Barbara Pariente, Peggy Quince, and Fred Lewis), an effort that was countered by a pro-retention group, Defend Justice from Politics. To account for this election-level factor, we include a control variable for campaigns that is coded 1 for the five races where anti-retention campaigns were mounted and 0 otherwise. Recall that Olson (2001) found that organized opposition led to lower vote totals for targeted judges.

To evaluate the possibility that voters may be more swayed by race and gender in low-salience retention elections, we include a dichotomous indicator for the race of the retention candidate (1 = white, 0 = nonwhite) and the gender of the candidate (1 = male, 0 = female). Given the possibility that the race of the candidate could affect white and nonwhite respondents differently (and likewise candidate gender may affect men and women differently), we interact the race of the candidate with the race of the respondent and the gender of the candidate with the gender of the respondent.[9] This allows us to determine not only whether women and minority candidates fare better or worse than white and/or male candidates, but also whether individuals are more likely to support a candidate who shares their demographic characteristics.

TABLE 5.3 Probit model of vote choice in retention elections

	COEFFICIENT (STANDARD ERROR)
Judge Democrat	0.300 (0.215)
Voter Democrat	0.667* (0.184)
Judge Democrat × Voter Democrat	0.047 (0.229)
Voter Republican	0.113 (0.176)
Judge Democrat × Voter Republican	−0.444* (0.221)
Previously retained	−0.081 (0.077)
Chief judge	0.055 (0.200)
Anti-retention campaign	0.013 (0.076)
Judge male	−0.043 (0.111)
Voter male	−0.131 (0.103)
Judge male × Voter male	0.034 (0.130)
Judge white	0.148 (0.250)
Voter white	0.037 (0.245)
Judge white × Voter white	−0.187 (0.262)
Constant	0.109 (0.309)
χ^2	209.22 ($p < 0.001$)
McKelvey/Zavoina r^2	0.165
n	4884

Notes: $^*p < 0.05$, two-tailed. The statistical significance of an interaction term is not determined by the z-test presented here; we evaluate the significance of the interactions separately in table 5.4.

Results of the probit model estimation appear in table 5.3. We begin interpreting the results by evaluating the effect of partisanship on vote choice in retention elections. The interpretation of interaction terms in nonlinear models is not straightforward (Ai and Norton 2003). This is simplified by computing discrete changes in the predicted probability of a "yes" vote under a variety of different scenarios. We take this approach in table 5.4, where we display predicted probabilities of Democrats and Republicans voting "yes" conditional on the judges' partisanship and holding all other variables constant at their modal values.

TABLE 5.4 Predicted probabilities of voting "yes" in retention elections

	PREDICTION	STANDARD ERROR	95% CONFIDENCE INTERVAL
Democrat for Democratic judge	0.852*	0.061	(0.732, 0.972)
Democrat for Republican judge	0.757*	0.084	(0.592, 0.922)
Difference	0.095*	0.041	(0.015, 0.174)
Republican for Democratic judge	0.500*	0.107	(0.290, 0.710)
Republican for Republican judge	0.671*	0.120	(0.436, 0.907)
Difference	−0.171*	0.081	(−0.331, 0.012)

Note: *$p < 0.05$, two-tailed. Figures are based on calculations from the model presented in table 5.3.

Perhaps the most striking aspect of table 5.4 is the relatively high probability of voting "yes" under any circumstances. The only category where the predicted probability of a yes vote falls below 0.5 is the category of Republicans voting for a Democratic judge, and even then the margin is only ever so slightly below 0.5. Generally speaking, voters are predisposed to keep current judges on the bench. Notwithstanding the general propensity to vote to retain the incumbent judge, partisan effects do emerge. A Democrat voting for a Democratic judge has a predicted probability of voting yes of 0.852, while a Democrat voting for a Republican judge has a predicted probability of voting yes at only 0.757. This difference of about 10% in the chances of voting yes is statistically significant at the $p < 0.05$ level. A Republican voting for a Democratic judge has a predicted probability of voting yes of 0.500; for a Republican voting for a Republican judge, the probability increases to 0.671. This difference, about 0.171, is also statistically significant.

Several possible reasons exist for greater partisan discrimination among Republicans than Democrats. One possibility is that the storied Republican distrust of federal courts may extend to state courts as well. A second possibility is that the anti-retention campaigns waged against judges came from the political right in 2012, and while we find no general direct effect of these campaigns, the campaigns may make it easier for Republicans to bring their partisanship to bear on their retention election voting decisions.

Measured against the pronounced effects of partisanship observed in contestable elections earlier in the manuscript, these effects may seem modest. However, on another level, it is remarkable that partisanship still exerts effects on election outcomes even in a nonpartisan election without campaigning and without an opponent. On this level, our results are consistent with the findings of Hall (2001) and Savchak and Barghothi (2007), who found that retention elections do not fully insulate judges from political pressures.

While partisanship may exert moderate but significant effects on vote choice in retention elections, we surprisingly find that anti-retention campaigns have little or no effect on the probability of a judge being retained, contrary to Olson (2001). While several judges in our sample were attacked for decisions made prior to their 2012 retention bid, our model finds these campaigns had no statistically significant effect on voters' propensity to vote "yes" on retention. From the information we have at hand, it is difficult to discern why these campaigns had no effect. It may be that the campaigns were of a relatively small magnitude or failed to capture the attention of voters, or that the anti-retention campaign was effectively countered by the pro-retention responses from candidates or groups that support them. Alternatively, the issues addressed in the campaigns may have concerned only a very small share of the electorate. In any event, these judges seemed to be isolated in large measure from the pressures these campaigns placed on them.

The model shows that previous success in a retention election has no significant influence on the probability of a "yes" vote in a retention election, nor does service as chief judge.

Even when using appropriate tests of significance for interaction terms in nonlinear models, we find no statistically significant effects of race. Simply put, for any combination of white or nonwhite voters and white or nonwhite judges, we find no statistically significant difference in the probability of voting "yes" on retention. In short, race figures little into voting in the elections we examined. Because our estimates may be less generalizable outside the context of the elections we examined, we should note that the nonwhite judges in our sample were all African Americans, so the effects could differ for other nonwhite judges. Additionally, none of the judges in our sample had uniquely ethnic names, so it is possible that voters simply had no knowledge of the race of the candidates when they were voting to retain them.

Similarly, we found no evidence that men were more or less likely to vote for male judges or that women were more or less likely to vote for female judges. The lone effect that we uncovered for gender is that men are across the board more likely to vote "no" on retention than women—this effect is as pronounced with a male judge as it is with a female judge. The names of the women in our sample likely sent clear signals about their gender, which gives us a high degree of confidence in our conclusion that voters are not influenced in their voting choices in retention elections by candidate gender.

Conclusion

Retention elections are intended as a balance between the accountability-inducing contestable election format and the independence of the appointment format. Our findings in this chapter suggest that retention election candidates tend to be on the whole very successful at winning votes. While they are not entirely immune from partisan pressures (Democrats vote for Democratic judges and Republicans vote for Republican judges), for most voters the default behavior seems to be to simply vote "yes."

In terms of normative implications, while the modest response to voters' preferences seems to reflect some degree of accountability, the general tendency to vote "yes" may mean that judges who face retention elections have a rather long electoral leash. This is seen by the infrequency with which judges lose their bids for retention and is supported by the fact that judges who were targeted for defeat by organized groups in 2012 did not experience a decrease in their vote total compared to those judges who were not targeted. Generally, our results do not show any evidence of accountability in retention elections and instead reveal a propensity for voters to simply keep the current officeholders. Given that scholars have not found any difference in quality between judges on the basis of selection system (e.g., Choi, Gulati, and Posner 2010), there is no reason to think that incumbents in retention states are more deserving of their jobs than their colleagues in partisan and nonpartisan states.

Finally, participation in retention elections remains below the levels typically seen in partisan elections, though retention elections actually fare better than nonpartisan elections in levels of participation, approximately on par with quasi-partisan elections. Still, with more than one in five voters rolling-off the ballot, retention elections leave something to be desired in terms of voter participation.

CONCLUSION

> *As with all such reforms, it will be necessary to develop well-crafted policies that set up appropriate incentives for all who are involved in the process.*
>
> —Rebecca D. Gill, "Beyond High Hopes and Unmet Expectations: Judicial Selection Reforms in the States"

In this book, we have explored the individual-level causes of voter participation and vote choice in state supreme court elections, the influences of ballot cues (such as partisan affiliation and incumbency status) on these choices, and the interactions between individual-level factors and ballot cues. After briefly summarizing our empirical results, we propose a shift in the judicial selection debate from accountability versus independence to transparency versus nontransparency, examine the implications of our results for lower court elections, speculate about future challenges and ongoing issues in the conduct of state supreme court elections, and, finally, take a step back and discuss how our results speak to some proposed reforms currently being debated in state legislatures.

Summary of Empirical Results

In chapter 1, we examined the consequences of partisan ballot labels on voter participation. Consistent with other scholars who examined aggregate data, we found that individuals in partisan elections participated at significantly higher rates than those in nonpartisan elections. We also separated out two states (Michigan and Ohio) that nominate candidates in partisan processes but that do not provide partisan labels on the general election ballot, and found that these states have higher levels of participation compared to purely nonpartisan states, but lower levels than partisan states.

We turned our attention to vote choice in chapter 2. Using observational data from the 2010 and 2012 CCES, we found that nonpartisan elections were ineffective at removing partisan considerations from voters' choice. That is, voters in nonpartisan elections were typically able to identify which of the candidates shared their partisan affiliation and supported those candidates at higher levels than their opponents.

We tested the mechanism behind that finding in chapter 3, where we conducted laboratory experiments to try to ascertain why partisan voting continues at high levels in nonpartisan elections. Our two experiments varied in the strength of the partisan signal we sent to the subjects. In one, it was quite clear which candidate was the Democrat and which was the Republican, even though we did not provide that information to the treatment group. In the other, the signals were far more muted, which may resemble the actual signal a voter receives given the other "clutter" that surrounds an actual campaign. When the signal is strong, voters were able to identify the candidate who is their co-partisan; when there was no signal or the signal was weak, partisanship had less effect on vote choice. We found that when issue-oriented information about candidates is available, the explicit use of partisan labels was unnecessary to facilitate partisan voting. In the absence of issue-oriented information, though, voters are at a loss for which candidate to select.

When taken together, the results of chapters 1–3 suggest that voters in nonpartisan elections who are unable to discern the partisanship of the candidates opt not to participate, leaving only voters who have a reasonable level of awareness of the candidates' partisan proclivities. The net result is lower participation in nonpartisan elections, though voters still have a strong partisan or ideological element among those who participate.

Chapter 4 focused on another key ballot cue: incumbency. Some states denote which candidate (if any) is the incumbent on the ballot. We posited that this might be one source of the incumbency advantage in state supreme court elections. Looking at both observational and experimental data, however, we found that the incumbency cue was simply not a significant predictor of vote choice. This was true even in nonpartisan elections, where it was the only ballot cue voters had. We do not suggest that incumbency is unimportant. A host of structural advantages in terms of running an effective campaign, a developed fund-raising network, name recognition, and more combine to give incumbents a formidable electoral advantage. Our results do suggest, however, that voters do not presume that all else being equal, an incumbent is a better candidate than a nonincumbent.

Finally, chapter 5 examined voter participation and vote choice in retention elections. We found that voters were more likely to participate in these elections compared to nonpartisan elections. Apparently, in a low-information environment, simply deciding whether to keep a judge is an easier decision than deciding among multiple candidates. There was also a "yes" vote bias; voters were predisposed to retain the current judges. That said, partisanship was also a significant factor: Democrats were more likely to vote for Democratic judges, and Republicans were more likely to vote for Republican judges. While the modest response to voters' preferences seems to reflect some degree of accountability, the general tendency to vote "yes" may mean that judges who face retention elections have a rather long electoral leash. This is seen by the infrequency with which judges lose their bids for retention.

Taken together, our results show the importance of partisanship and partisan cues in all types of elections: partisan, quasi-partisan, nonpartisan, and retention. Partisanship is the only ballot cue that seems to matter; the incumbency cue is irrelevant. We find no empirical basis for the claim made by proponents of nonpartisan elections that these elections are able to remove partisan considerations from voting. While the effect may be weaker, one can even demonstrate meaningful partisan influences on vote choice in retention elections. Our results suggest that regardless of the type of election, in state supreme court races voters are able to identify their co-partisans and support them in high numbers.

From Independence versus Accountability to Transparency versus Nontransparency

Historically, the debate over different methods of selection has been between those who advocate for judicial independence (appointment) and those who argue for judicial accountability (elections). Interestingly, judicial elections were initially proposed (and supported) as a way to promote judicial independence and reduce the politics involved in judicial selection (Shugerman 2012). So-called merit selection was proposed as a way to provide for both of these, though, as we discussed in chapter 5, it is imperfect at providing for either. To a large extent, this debate has grown stale; all judges are both independent and accountable, though to different constituencies (see Gill 2013 for a good discussion on this point). "In the switch from one form of selection to another, judges become more independent from one set of powers but more accountable to another" (Shugerman 2012, 7). Indeed, even those who have traditionally defended judicial independence note that "the legal establishment has painted itself into a corner by defending the need for judicial independence with almost exclusive reference to an implausible claim . . . that independent judges do not make rules of law but merely follow them (Geyh 2012, 625–26). Interestingly, Geyh (2014, 5) reports that "organizations devoted to promoting judicial independence have discovered that the term 'judicial independence' plays poorly with the public (because 'independence' is equated with 'unaccountability')."

One of the problems in the judicial independence literature is a lack of clarity over what is meant by the term. Indeed, Kornhauser (2002, 51) argues that because of this lack of clarity, "the concept of judicial independence is not useful." Disagreeing with this pessimistic conclusion, Geyh (2014) develops a typology that he uses to organize the research on judicial independence and also move it forward in important ways. For Geyh, the notion of "unqualified judicial independence" is simply either a slogan or a straw man. No serious scholar believes that judges should have complete and total independence. However, judicial independence can be a useful concept if we think about it in terms of behavioral independence and structural independence. Importantly, just because institutions are designed to promote judicial independence does not mean that judges will behave independently.

Geyh argues that judges make policy, but they make policy in different ways than legislators, and this is one reason why they are deserving of some degree of judicial independence. That is, "if . . . the 'law' means whatever the political majority tells judges it means at any given moment in time, then the rule of law constrains neither judicial decision-making nor the political branches and is replaced by unvarnished power politics" (Geyh 2005, 899). However, much like those who argue for unqualified judicial independence, this argument is a straw man; clearly judges, at least in some cases, are constrained by the rules and norms of the political system. If nothing else, judges are bound to consider the law and frame their decisions and opinions with respect to what the law says (or is alleged to say). Thus, Geyh argues that we need to strike a balance between "which selection option under consideration optimizes 'good' independence that enables judges to follow due process, administer pragmatic justice, and uphold the rule of law, while minimizing 'bad' independence that liberates judges to disregard these same three objectives" (Geyh 2012, 630). He argues that we need to move beyond sweeping polemics and proposals for reform and focus instead on incremental, moderate reforms that can improve the existing method of selection in the states (whatever it is) to allow for both independence and accountability.

There is considerable merit to Geyh's argument, and we think this approach is likely to be useful to scholars of both law and courts. However, we think that an exclusive focus on judicial independence is inadequate and ignores an important component of judicial politics: many judges are dependent on the public (either directly or indirectly) to achieve and retain their position. To be sure, judicial independence is implicated in this, but the constant need to face the public implicates more than just the concept of independence. Thus, we suggest that instead of just focusing on judicial accountability and judicial independence, a focus on transparency is also a useful and important way to evaluate methods of selection.

In a democracy, we should prefer systems that are more transparent to those that are less transparent. On this score, elections currently fare the best: voters are involved in both the selection of candidates and in determining which candidates win. In the words of Shugerman (2012, 5): "With direct popular elections, we watch the sausage-making. With appointments, the sausage-making is out of sight, out of mind." But this need not be the case. Certainly, appointment systems can be made more transparent, with more public input into the nominees and public vetting of candidates. In states that utilize Judicial Performance Evaluations (JPEs), releasing the raw data and making public the methodology used to derive recommendations would also go a long way toward improving the transparency of the system. Another way to increase transparency would be to involve the public in the selection of people for the judicial nominating commissions (JNCs). Instead of vesting this appointment power in the hands of political and legal elites, why not have the public involved in the selection? This would insure that the public's views are represented and that the system is not simply dominated by elites who may not share the preferences of the public (see Fitzpatrick 2009).[1] The argument against this is that the public does not know enough to make decisions about which candidates are most qualified, and if you get unqualified people on the selection committee, they may nominate less qualified individuals for judgeships. However, this presupposes that JNCs make nominations solely on the basis of qualifications, and there is ample evidence that this is false (e.g., Fitzpatrick 2009). Indeed, it is well known that "appointing authorities, be they Presidents, legislatures, or Governors do not focus exclusively on merit in selecting individuals for judgeships" (Dimino 2005, 295).

Of course, even among states that select judges via appointment (for purposes of this discussion we include "merit selection" states because the initial selection is by appointment), there is considerable variation in transparency. For example, in Oklahoma the public is completely shut out of the process. The commission meetings, interviews, and deliberations are all conducted privately. On the other hand, in Arizona, notice of the meetings is posted and not only is the public invited, but there is also an opportunity for the public to comment on potential nominees. After the meeting, the minutes of the meeting are posted on the commission's website. These are important components of the system even if they are simply "done for show" as "people have . . . been found to value the opportunity to express their views to decision-makers in situations in which they believe that what they are saying has little or no influence upon the decisions being made" (Tyler 2000, 121). Clearly, the system in Arizona is more transparent than the system utilized in Oklahoma. Unfortunately, as these two examples illustrate, retention states vary widely in how transparent they are.

While states that appoint judges may be somewhat less transparent than elected states (if only because public involvement is less extensive), there are ways to improve the transparency of all systems. The more transparent the system is, the more legitimate it is likely to be. Thus, since all judges are both independent and accountable (though to different constituencies), it makes more sense to view (and evaluate) selection systems based on how transparent they are to the public. We should be more skeptical of systems that seek to limit public involvement in the decision-making process. This is a recipe for decisions being made on the basis of factors other than merit (Fitzpatrick 2009).

Implications for Lower Courts

All of the data we presented in this book are from state supreme court elections. While these are enormously important offices, they represent a small fraction of elected judges in the United States. The lion's share of elected judges serve in intermediate appellate courts, general jurisdiction trial courts, and limited jurisdiction trial courts. Thus far, elections for these courts have been largely immune from high rates of contestation, electoral competition, campaign spending, and advertising that characterize modern state supreme court elections (Arbour and McKenzie 2010, 2011; Frederick 2008, 2011; M. Nelson 2011; Streb and Frederick 2009, 2011; Streb, Frederick, and LaFrance 2007, 2009).

We would expect ballot cues to be even more important in these types of elections. While state supreme court elections are characterized by high levels of contestation, competition, and campaign spending, this is not true of lower court elections. Absent vigorous campaigns, the cues presented to voters on the ballots themselves are likely to take on increasing importance. Our experimental results in chapter 3 certainly suggest that this is the case, and even the ballot cue of incumbency, which we found did not matter at the state supreme court level in chapter 4, may be relevant in elections for lower court seats. However, if these races become more expensive and more competitive, they may begin to resemble state supreme court races. We are interested in future studies that evaluate whether there are differences in the determinants of voter participation, competitive races, and so forth among lower court races that are hotly contested versus those that are not. Based on what we have found at the state supreme court level in this volume, it seems competitive races are governed by different factors than noncompetitive races.

At the same time, the lower salience and "sleepy" nature of these races means that many voters will simply not participate in them. Scholars of both intermediate appellate courts (Streb and Frederick 2011; Streb, Frederick, and LaFrance 2009) and trial courts (M. Nelson 2011) have found ballot roll-off to be significantly higher in these elections compared to state supreme court elections. Unsurprisingly, partisan elections continue to have higher levels of voter participation, just as in state supreme court elections.

This points to the need for individual-level data for decisions made by voters in lower court elections. These courts are the workhorses of the judicial system and are indispensable for the efficient administration of justice. Understanding how voters (and candidates) behave in these elections is essential for scholars to have a complete picture of the conduct of judicial elections. It is important for us to know which of our findings are limited to the state high court context and which are true of judicial elections more generally. Indeed, the results of such inquiry could lead scholars (and policymakers) to support one form of election for state supreme courts and a different method of selection for lower courts.

Ongoing Issues and Future Challenges

Given institutional inertia and the high level of public support, judicial elections are not going away anytime soon. We want to revisit three issues that will help (re)define the landscape of judicial elections over the next several years: public finance, independent expenditures, and legitimacy.

PUBLIC FINANCE

As mentioned in the introduction, the fate of effective public financing of judicial campaigns is in question after the Supreme

Court's decision in *Arizona Free Enterprise Club's Freedom Club PAC v. Bennett.* Moreover, the most successful public financing system to date (North Carolina) has been eliminated (Clark 2013; Huffstetler 2013). Given the success of the North Carolina system, and the fact that the public is concerned about campaign contributions affecting the legitimacy of state courts (Gibson 2012; Cann and Yates 2008), this is an unwelcome development.

Interestingly, while North Carolina eliminated their public financing system, West Virginia recently voted to strengthen theirs. In 2012, West Virginia had a pilot program for public financing, and only one of the four candidates took advantage of it (O'Brien 2013). This candidate won one of the two open seats in the election despite receiving only $350,000 in public funds. In the 2016 elections, candidates will receive $300,000 for a contested primary and $525,000 for a contested general election (Kabler 2013), with no provision for "rescue funds" in order to comply with the U.S. Supreme Court ruling in *Bennett.* These are still relatively modest sums; on average, candidates spent $958,824 in the 2012 general election for the West Virginia high court (excluding Allen Loughry, the publicly financed candidate), with two candidates spending over $1.2 million. Given these circumstances, only time will tell how many candidates (if any) will opt to use public financing. If candidates who choose public financing continue to be at a significant financial disadvantage in the election, it is difficult to see the public financing scheme becoming popular with candidates.

Additionally, Kentucky is considering adopting public financing of judicial campaigns. A bill patterned after the North Carolina law (but without the rescue funds) passed the Kentucky legislature in 2013, though it was not considered by the state senate before the legislative term expired (Musgrave 2013). While this proposal faces an uphill battle in terms of its likelihood of success, the fact that it is being discussed suggests that legislators continue to be concerned with the funding of elections and are willing to consider public financing as an alternative to the status quo. In times of tight budgets, it is unclear how many additional states will take up the issue of public funding or, even if they adopt a public financing system, how much money states will be able to provide to candidates. This issue is certainly one worth monitoring, particularly since state supreme court races are not becoming any less expensive.

INDEPENDENT EXPENDITURES

All of the focus on public financing assumes that campaign spending by the candidates themselves is the most important source of spending. However, over the past decade, there has been a large increase in both the frequency and the amount of spending by independent interest groups (Bannon et al. 2013). This spending occurs outside of the candidates' campaigns and, due to state disclosure laws, is incredibly difficult to track reliably.

To the extent that this spending continues to represent a sizable proportion of spending on campaigns, models that use official reports by the candidates likely understate the amount of spending. That said, there is a trade-off in terms of reliability since candidates are required by law to disclose their amount of spending, and many independent groups do not have this requirement. It is easier (and more straightforward) to get replicable data from official reports filed by candidates. Additionally, while relying on candidate spending reports undercounts the amount of spending, there is no reason, a priori, to think this measure is biased in favor of one candidate (or type of candidate) since all candidates will be operating under the same rules.

The rise of independent expenditures is also an opportunity for scholars to test interesting hypotheses about who receives this type of funding, if the type of independent group varies by state (or by election within a state), if the same groups appear in multiple election cycles, if they are limited to just one candidate, and so on. Answers to all of these questions are currently unknown and would contribute to our understanding of the role of money in judicial elections.

PERCEPTIONS OF LEGITIMACY

Scholars have yet to complete wrestling with the relationship between judicial selection and legitimacy. A basic tension exists between the well-established findings of different scholars. First, Gibson (2012) uses compelling evidence from both experiments and observational data to argue that elections do not erode the legitimacy of the judicial system. Second, though, it is also clear that the public is concerned about the appearance of impropriety with judges making decisions in a way that benefits their campaign contributors (e.g., Iyengar 2002; Persily and Lammie 2004). These two well-argued and factually supported claims seem to be at odds with each other: if the public thinks elected judges are behaving in a way that benefits their contributors, how does this not lead to a decrease in the legitimacy of courts?

There are two possible explanations for this tension, though determining which (if either) is correct will require scholars to think creatively both in terms of research design and execution. First, it could be that contentious campaigns and large amounts of campaign contributions will have effects on legitimacy only in the long run. Given the relative recent appearances of these factors in most states, it may be too soon to see any effects on legitimacy. Indeed, one of the reasons that Gibson (2012) chose to analyze Kentucky is because elections there were competitive and contested, but this type of salient campaigning is a relatively recent phenomenon. While Gibson's work is an important and invaluable first look at this issue, it should not be regarded as the last word.

Second, it may be that the effects of campaigns on legitimacy have already been felt. This may explain why Cann and Yates (2008) and Benesh (2006) find that individuals in partisan election states hold their courts in lower esteem than those in states using other selection methods. If this is true, then it makes sense that contemporary elections do not continue to erode the legitimacy of courts; the costs have already been paid. This implies that if a state currently using a selection system other than partisan elections were to shift to a partisan election system, there would be a loss of legitimacy. Unfortunately, testing this hypothesis requires longitudinal data that we currently do not have. As states consider changing their method of selection (for example, if North Carolina were to switch back to partisan elections from nonpartisan elections), scholars might have the analytical leverage needed to test this hypothesis.

Relatedly, there is an open question of whether even *proposing* reform can affect the legitimacy of courts. Generally speaking, when politicians and interest groups propose tinkering with institutional design, it is because they want to improve outcomes beneficial to them. It may be the case that proposals to change methods of judicial selection, even if unsuccessful, can have a deleterious effect on judicial legitimacy. With all the proposals for change currently being floated in several states that we discuss in the next section, this is a topic that is ripe for investigation.

Other Proposed Reforms

In addition to the three issues discussed above, states are considering several other reforms to their system of judicial selection. While most of these are still proposals, if any of them are adopted they will drastically change the nature of judicial selection in the state. The sheer number of proposals for reform is surprisingly high and is not limited to one method of selection. Indeed, there seems to be a high level of dissatisfaction (at least from some factions) with the status quo. Many of these proposals involve the state legislature trying to reclaim some of the power currently held by JNCs. Here, we briefly discuss the proposals and the likely consequences. All this emphasizes the need for the continued study of judicial selection and the need for both scholars and policymakers to carefully consider the implications of any institutional changes that are proposed. As our empirical results presented earlier demonstrated, there are often unintended consequences that arise from institutional reforms.

Arizona. In 2012, voters in Arizona rejected Proposition 115, which would have changed the state constitution to require judicial nominating commissions to send at least five names to the governor instead of the three-name list that is currently required. This was defeated by a nearly 3:1 margin. Despite this, in February 2013, the state legislature passed a bill (signed by the governor) to require at least five names to be presented to the governor. Given that the state constitution states that only three names must be given to the governor, it is not surprising that this law was struck down by the Arizona Supreme Court in September 2013 (Fischer 2013). Supporters of the change are considering proposing another amendment for the 2014 elections. Obviously, if such a change would be successful, it would give the governor more flexibility in choosing a judge of his or her liking. This would dilute the agenda-setting authority of the commission and reduce their role in the process. The fewer names the commission has to recommend, the more powerful it is.

Florida. Voters in Florida decisively rejected (with 65% of the vote) an attempt to give the legislature more say in the operation of the Florida Supreme Court (Olorunnipa and Davis 2012). Proposition 5 would have allowed the legislature to change a rule of the court by a simple majority vote (instead of the two-thirds majority currently required by the state constitution) and would require the governor's appointments to this court (from a list generated by a judicial nominating commission) to be subjected to senate confirmation. In 2013, the House passed Bill 7033, which allows for the removal of any member of a JNC at any time without cause (Schorsch 2013). As in the case of Arizona, this would give increased power to the governor and diminish the power of the JNC. One could argue that this is a good thing since the governor is elected and accountable to the people, while the JNC is accountable to no one. On the other hand, one could also argue that this makes the commission (and therefore the courts) less independent by subjecting them to control by the governor.

Georgia. As in most states that utilize judicial elections, when there is a vacancy on a court in Georgia, the governor is authorized to appoint a replacement. However, HB 30 would set up a JNC for this purpose and would require the governor to select a candidate from the list generated by the commission (Raftery 2013). Interestingly, there is no minimum or maximum number of names the commission has to send to the governor, so presumably the commission could provide the governor with only one name, effectively taking over the selection process from the governor. This bill is still pending in the House.

Illinois. In Illinois, there are two proposals to change the current method of partisan elections and the retention elections after the initial term. One proposal would waive the need for retention elections if judges are determined by a commission to be performing their duties well. If judges are rated unsatisfactory, they would need to stand for retention (Moser 2013). Needless to say, this would take the power away from voters and place it in the hands of an unaccountable commission. Indeed, the voters would only have a say if this commission determined a judge was bad enough to face the voters. A second proposal would require all judges and judicial candidates to obtain the support of a special commission before even appearing on the ballot, and then would require a two-thirds vote to keep their jobs, up from the current 60 percent (*Chicago Tribune* 2013). Again, this reform would allow voters to participate in the selection and retention process only after a commission has determined that that candidates/judges are qualified. It is thought that both of these proposals are long shots to be enacted.

Indiana. Legislators in Indiana are proposing to require the governor to select non-attorney members from a list generated by the state legislature for the JNC (J. Nelson 2013). Currently, the governor is unconstrained in his or her choice of non-attorney members. Indiana requires three of the seven members of the JNC to be nonlawyers (Fitzpatrick 2009). This is an attempt by the legislature to exert influence on the composition of the selection committee. This probably would not erode the commission's independence, since the governor currently has complete control over the non-attorney members; this would merely put some legislative constraints on the governor's appointment power over some of the commission members.

Kansas. In Kansas, both the governor and a significant proportion of the state legislature support moving from so-called merit selection to gubernatorial appointment with senate confirmation. Indeed, this has already been done for the Kansas intermediate appellate court, which only required changing a law as opposed to amending the state constitution (Carpenter 2013). To change the method of selection for the Kansas Supreme Court, reformers would need two-thirds of both houses of the legislature plus a majority of voters in a statewide election (Hanna 2013). This proposal has already made it through the state senate (Milburn 2013). By moving away from a commission-based model to a model identical to the federal model of selection, power would be shifted to the governor and the senate at the expense of the JNC. Similar to the proposal in Arizona, it is unclear what the effects of such a move would be.

Minnesota. Minnesota is once again considering moving from nonpartisan elections to a system of commission nomination, gubernatorial appointment, and retention elections. This proposal has been discussed since an independent commission chaired by former governor Al Quie recommended moving to a merit selection system in 2007. As in the past, the proposal is not poised to pass in the state legislature (Helgeson 2013). However, given that this proposal has been defeated in the past and continues to resurface, it seems unlikely that proponents of reform in Minnesota will abandon the proposal. Interestingly, Minnesota ranks near the bottom of states that elect judges on just about every measure of competitiveness and contestation, indicating that most races are uncontested, and those that are contested are not competitive or expensive (Bonneau 2007a). Perhaps one reason why the reform has not gained much traction is that legislators and citizens do not perceive that the current method of selection is problematic.

Montana. A legislator in Montana has introduced a bill requiring state supreme court justices to have prior experience as a lower court judge (Gouras 2013). Given that Bonneau and Hall (2009; Hall and Bonneau 2006) have shown that challengers to state supreme court incumbents who have prior judicial experience perform better than challengers who do not, this requirement might lead to more competitive races in Montana. At present, the proposal lacks the support necessary for passage.

North Carolina. As mentioned above, North Carolina eliminated public financing for its elections and is considering switching back to partisan elections from nonpartisan elections. A return to partisan elections would allow for an interesting research design to examine the effects of this change. Since moving to nonpartisan elections, North Carolina state supreme court races have experienced lower levels of voter participation and electoral competition (Bonneau and Hall 2009).

Ohio. Ohio chief justice Maureen O'Connor has been promoting an eight-point plan for reforming and improving the Ohio court system. Her plan does not propose to eliminate judicial elections, acknowledging that they are quite popular with citizens (M. O'Connor 2013). She focuses instead on issues such as having elections in odd-numbered years, eliminating partisan primaries, increasing the length of the term of office, and having a commission recommend people to fill vacancies. A detailed analysis of her plan is outside the scope of this conclusion, especially since it is unclear whether the state legislature will take up any of her suggestions. However, given the historic competitiveness of state supreme court elections in Ohio, any changes to the status quo (other than a shift from quasi-partisan to partisan elections) would likely lead to less competitiveness.

Oklahoma. In Oklahoma, the state senate passed a bill limiting state supreme court justices to a single, twenty-year term of office (McNutt 2013). This bill was not taken up in the House, but the

House has launched a study to examine how members of the appellate bench should be chosen. In addition to the single, twenty-year term of office, reformers are advocating moving from the current system of "merit" selection to either the federal system (where the governor would nominate a candidate and the state senate would confirm him or her) or a system of competitive judicial elections (Associated Press 2013). Moving to either of these would increase the accountability of judges either directly (via elections) or indirectly (via gubernatorial selection and legislative confirmation). Of course, having judges serve only a single term would certainly mitigate this move toward greater accountability, since judges with no opportunity to retain their position at the end of their term would have no constraints on their behavior and would be free to decide cases any way they chose.

Pennsylvania. Pennsylvania is once again considering eliminating partisan elections for judges' initial terms.[2] The reform proposal would require the governor to select a judge from a list of five names provided by a JNC, and this nomination would be subject to confirmation by the state senate (Mondics 2013). A similar proposal has been floated in the past. In order to amend the state constitution to change the method of selection, the proposal must pass both legislative houses in two consecutive sessions and then be approved by the voters. This is no small feat. While this is unlikely to pass, it has received support from a bipartisan group of four former governors (*Erie Times-News* 2013). Such a shift would almost certainly reduce participation in Pennsylvania judicial elections.

South Carolina. South Carolina, one of the two states that select judges by the legislature, is considering a minor reform to their approach. Currently, the Judicial Merit Selection Committee (JMSC) presents the state legislature with the names of three candidates, and the legislature is forced to decide among them. Under the reform, the commission would remain in place to screen candidates to ensure that they are qualified under state law to serve, but it would then forward all of the qualified names to the legislature (WACH FOX 2013). This would decrease the commission's agenda-setting power, giving more discretion to the state legislature. It is unclear what effect this would have on the types of candidates selected since the legislature currently selects all ten members of the JMSC, and six of the ten members are sitting legislators. Thus, the legislature is already deeply involved in the screening and selection process.

South Dakota. In South Dakota, the JNC responsible for recommending candidates for vacancies may be expanded from seven members to nine. Currently, the governor appoints two members, the judicial branch appoints two members, and the state bar appoints three members. Under SB198, the legislature would appoint two members of the commission as well (Mercer 2013). This would weaken the influence of the state bar association.

As the above list demonstrates, the issue of judicial selection is very timely and salient in many states. Most of the proposed reforms involve increasing the role of the elected branches of government (governor and legislature) at the expense of the state bar association and independent (and unaccountable) JNCs. Additionally, states that elect their judges in competitive elections continue to receive criticism. In fact, the only system currently immune from efforts at reform is gubernatorial appointment (sometimes with legislative confirmation). Over time, different selections systems have been in vogue, beginning with gubernatorial appointment, moving to partisan elections, to nonpartisan elections, to the merit system, and now seemingly back to gubernatorial appointment.

Conclusion

Courts serve a variety of crucially important roles in a functioning democracy. State supreme courts stand out as particularly important players in the American court system for their role as the final arbiters on matters of state law as well as for the volume of cases they adjudicate. Given the vital importance of state courts in the American political system, the means by which these judges are selected and retained is a matter of great importance.

Decades of political science research have demonstrated the remarkable influence of party identification on political behavior in a wide range of settings. Our research demonstrates that, rather remarkably, the influence of party identification is pronounced even in the face of electoral formats designed with the specific goal of eliminating partisan influence. Indeed, we see one of the most important contributions of our work in this volume to be our results demonstrating the remarkable influence of party identification across a wide range of electoral formats.

Effective policy analysis requires a unique combination of choosing values (selecting outcomes we deem to be "good") and using empirical evaluation techniques to determine whether a particular policy is effective at producing the outcomes one values. Analyzing policies governing judicial selection and retention is no exception. To the extent that one holds political participation as a value, our results suggest that partisan elections excel in this area, with relatively few voters electing to skip partisan judicial races; contestable nonpartisan races fare relatively poorly on this front. Retention elections, while lagging behind partisan elections on this front, fare surprisingly well, performing on par with contestable quasi-partisan elections. The simplest reform states could enact to increase participation in judicial elections would be to switch to partisan elections.

To the extent that one holds minimizing the influence of partisanship and ideology in judicial selection as a value, one may suspect that partisan elections would be a poor choice. However, our results suggest nonpartisan elections are only modestly better, if they are better at all. While retention elections show less susceptibility to partisanship, even these elections without challengers are influenced by partisan considerations. These results suggest that there is, as yet, no available reform to truly eliminate the influence of partisanship from judicial selection.

We also offer the value of transparency as a criterion for evaluating judicial selection and retention policies. We see open, competitive electoral processes as inherently transparent, but as we discussed in evaluating proposed reforms in several states, a number of reform options exist for making systems that utilize JNC's and pure appointment systems more transparent.

Others may offer additional values to consider when considering the best system by which to select and retain judges. Many such values have been proposed, including systems that produce a diverse bench and judges who write clearer opinions (Hurwitz and Lanier 2003; Goelzhauser and Cann 2014). In the constraints of this volume, we would be stretched to discuss all values that could be sought in a judicial election system, much less provide empirical tests of which systems, if any, can achieve those goals. Instead, we conclude with an encouragement that future scholars not only carefully consider the values they seek in judicial selection systems, but also evaluate whether existing (or new) policies can actually achieve the values they are designed to promote.

APPENDIX A: ABOUT THE CCES

The Cooperative Congressional Election Study (CCES) is a national stratified sample survey of over fifty thousand people. The CCES is designed to allow individual scholars to receive survey content of their own making while also creating a core set of content that is of general interest to scholars studying American elections. Teams participate by purchasing a subset of one thousand respondents. The survey is fielded as a twenty-minute pre-election survey, and then respondents are contacted again to complete a ten-minute post-election survey. For both the pre- and post-election surveys, the first half of the questionnaire for all participating teams is devoted to common content. The common content covers respondents' basic demographic information, party affiliation, preferences on issues, vote choice in particular races, and a variety of attitudes toward elected officials.

The second half of the CCES questionnaire is devoted to team-specific content. This allows a participating team to pose original questions of their own making to a nationally representative sample of one thousand people. It is often possible to trade content across teams as well to increase the sample size for particular questions. For example, on the 2010 CCES, the common content asked for whom respondents voted in presidential, senatorial, congressional, gubernatorial, and state legislative races. However, the CCES did not ask about vote choice in state supreme court elections. In fact, prior to our efforts there was no national survey of voters in judicial elections. We placed vote choice for state supreme court on the Utah State and University of Pittsburgh modules of the CCES. Then we traded time on the Utah State team content questionnaire for time on another institution's team content. It might seem like this approach would yield three thousand responses to a question about vote choice in a state supreme court election. However, not all states elect their judges, so the state supreme court vote choice was not asked of those respondents. Additionally, not all states that elect judges had contested elections in 2010. Still, across the three modules, we were able to observe the decisions of voters' to participate in a judicial election for over one thousand respondents and the actual vote choice of about four hundred respondents.

As we disseminated the results of our work on the 2010 CCES, enthusiasm for the study of state supreme courts mounted, and the director of the CCES, Stephen Ansolabehere at Harvard University, invited us to propose state supreme court vote choice as a question for the common content in 2012. Because the vote choice question was asked of every CCES respondent on every team's module in 2012, we observed about five thousand vote choices of about ten thousand individuals who are eligible to vote in state supreme court elections in 2012.

The CCES is fielded online, but unlike most Internet surveys, stratification, matching, and weighting of the data yield a nationally representative sample. The methodology is detailed in Rivers (2007) and cross-validated by Ansolabehere and Schaffner (2011), who show that for a wide range of variables the population point estimates are similar for the CCES when compared to national mail and random-digit dial phone surveys. The online format also allows for simple incorporation of a variety of question types and graphics that cannot be included in a conventional survey over the phone.

APPENDIX B: LIST OF RACES INCLUDED IN THE STUDY

2010 Elections

The number of respondents reflects individuals who were asked about their participation (for tables 1.1 and 5.1) and vote choice (tables 2.3, 2.4, and 5.3) for each race. Note that particularly in Texas in 2010 (but also in other states), some of voters expressed, "I'm sure I voted in this race, but I can't remember which candidate I voted for," which made it possible to use their verified vote in table 1.1 but kept us from using their vote choice in tables 2.3 and 2.4. There is slight variation in sample sizes between table 2.3 and 2.5 due to missing values on ideology.

The election in Michigan is a multiseat race, where voters are permitted to vote for two candidates. We allowed respondents to choose two candidates.

STATE	CANDIDATES	NUMBER OF RESPONDENTS IN DIFFERENT ANALYSES
Alabama	Tom Parker Douglas "Mac" Parsons	Table 1.1: 21 Table 2.3: 7
Alabama	Kelli Wise Rhonda Chambers	Table 1.1: 21 Table 2.3: 7
Alabama	Michael Bolin Tom Edwards	Table 1.1: 21 Table 2.3: 7

STATE	CANDIDATES	NUMBER OF RESPONDENTS IN DIFFERENT ANALYSES
Arkansas	Karen Baker Tim Fox	Table 1.1: 18 Table 2.3: 8
Georgia	David Nahmias Matt Wilson Tammy Lynn Adkins	Table 1.1: 80 Table 2.3: 27
Michigan	Bob Young Alton Davis Thomas Mary Beth Kelly Denise Morris Robert Roddis	Table 1.1: 27 Table 2.3: —
Minnesota	Helen Meyer Greg Wersal	Table 1.1: 36 Table 2.3: 10
Minnesota	Alan Page Tim Tingelstad	Table 1.1: 37 Table 2.3: 21
Montana	Beth Baker Nels Swindal	Table 1.1: 8 Table 2.3: 4
North Carolina	Bob Hunter Barbara Jackson	Table 1.1: 61 Table 2.3: 22
Ohio	Judith Ann Lanzinger Mary Jane Trapp	Table 2.1: 90 Table 2.3: 58
Ohio	Eric Brown Maureen O'Connor	Table 1.1: 90 Table 2.3: 60
Texas	Eva Guzman Blake Bailey	Table 1.1: 109 Table 2.3: 20
Texas	Paul Green William Moody	Table 1.1: 113 Table 2.3: 24
Texas	Debra Lehrman Jim Sharp	Table 1.1: 115 Table 2.3: 26
Texas	Michael Keasler Keith Hampton	Table 1.1: 115 Table 2.3: 16
Washington	Richard Sanders Charlie Wiggins	Table 1.1: 67 Table 2.3: 37
West Virginia	Thomas McHugh John Yoder	Table 1.1: 17 Table 2.3: 77

2012 Elections

Illinois, Kentucky, Maryland, Mississippi, and Nebraska elect their state supreme court candidates in district-based elections. Because the CCES supreme court vote choice questions were asked of all respondents in each state, we have used only the responses for state supreme court elections for individuals who lived in the district to which these elections pertain. For example, the Illinois First Supreme Court District comprises Cook County. Even though respondents from all over Illinois may have been asked about this race, we only use responses from verified voters living in Cook County. In one state, Nebraska, the Fourth Supreme Court District does not follow county lines, so we were unable to determine which voters were actually eligible for this race to retain Michael McCormack. As a result, the Northeast Fourth District retention race is omitted from our analyses. Additionally, once respondents for the race between Earle Banks and William Waller who had not lived in the counties covered by the First District and individuals who were not verified to have voted were removed from the data, we were left with zero respondents in that district.

The elections in Michigan and West Virginia are multiseat races, where voters are permitted to vote for two candidates. We allowed respondents to choose two candidates.

STATE	CANDIDATES	NUMBER OF RESPONDENTS IN DIFFERENT ANALYSES
Alabama	Roy Moore Robert Vance	Table 1.1: 480 Table 2.3: 350 Table 5.1: 480 Table 5.3: —
Alaska	Daniel Winfree	Table 1.1: — Table 2.3: — Table 5.1: 82 Table 5.3: 66
Arizona	John Pelander	Table 1.1: — Table 2.3: — Table 5.1: 1020 Table 5.3: 548
Colorado	Nathan Coats	Table 1.1: — Table 2.3: — Table 5.1: 723 Table 5.3: 482

STATE	CANDIDATES	NUMBER OF RESPONDENTS IN DIFFERENT ANALYSES
Florida	Barbara Pariente	Table 1.1: — Table 2.3: — Table 5.1: 856 Table 5.3: 591
Florida	Fred Lewis	Table 1.1: — Table 2.3: — Table 5.1: 871 Table 5.3: 575
Florida	Peggy Quince	Table 1.1: — Table 2.3: — Table 5.1: 868 Table 5.3: 575
Illinois	Mary Jane Theis James G. Riley	Table 1.1: 469 Table 2.3: 326 Table 5.1: 469 Table 5.3: —
Indiana	Robert Rucker	Table 1.1: — Table 2.3: — Table 5.1: 378 Table 5.3: 218
Indiana	Steven David	Table 1.1: — Table 2.3: — Table 5.1: 362 Table 5.3: 219
Iowa	David Wiggins	Table 1.1: — Table 2.3: — Table 5.1: 107 Table 5.3: 85
Iowa	Edward Mansfield	Table 1.1: — Table 2.3: — Table 5.1: 142 Table 5.3: 98
Iowa	Bruce Zager	Table 1.1: — Table 2.3: — Table 5.1: 118 Table 5.3: 86
Iowa	Thomas Waterman	Table 1.1: — Table 3.3: — Table 5.1: 105 Table 5.3: 78

STATE	CANDIDATES	NUMBER OF RESPONDENTS IN DIFFERENT ANALYSES
Kansas	Nancy Caplinger-Moritz	Table 1.1: — Table 2.3: — Table 5.1: 507 Table 5.3: 316
Kentucky	William Scott Janet Stumbo	Table 1.1: 59 Table 2.3: 40 Table 5.1: 59 Table 5.3: —
Maine	Donald Alexander	Table 1.1: — Table 2.3: — Table 5.1: 135 Table 5.3: 31
Maine	Warren Silver	Table 1.1: — Table 2.3: — Table 5.1: 160 Table 5.3: 25
Maryland	Lynne Battaglia	Table 2.1: — Table 3.3: — Table 6.1: 47 Table 6.3: 29
Maryland	Robert M. Bell	Table 2.1: — Table 3.3: — Table 6.1: 19 Table 6.3: 14
Maryland	Robert N. McDonald	Table 2.1: — Table 3.3: — Table 6.1: 254 Table 6.3: 140
Michigan	Doug Dern Connie Marie Kelley Stephen Markman Bridget Mary McCormack Kerry Morgan Colleen O'Brien Bob Roddis	Table 1.1: 648 Table 2.3: — Table 5.1: 648 Table 5.3: —
Michigan	Mindy Barry Shelia Johnson Brian Zahra	Table 1.1: 610 Table 2.3: 350 Table 5.1: 610 Table 5.3: —

STATE	CANDIDATES	NUMBER OF RESPONDENTS IN DIFFERENT ANALYSES
Minnesota	Lorie Skjerven Gildea Dan Griffith	Table 1.1: 178 Table 2.3: — Table 5.1: 178 Table 5.3: —
Minnesota	Barry Anderson Dean Barkley	Table 1.1: 187 Table 2.3: — Table 5.1: 187 Table 5.3: —
Minnesota	David Stras Tim Tingelstad	Table 1.1: 165 Table 2.3: — Table 5.1: 165 Table 5.3: —
Mississippi	Josiah Dennis Coleman Richard (Flip) Phillips	Table 1.1: 17 Table 2.3: 14 Table 5.1: 17 Table 5.3: —
Mississippi	Talmadge Braddock Mike Randolph	Table 1.1: 28 Table 2.3: 22 Table 5.1: 28 Table 5.3: —
Montana	Laurie McKinnon Ed Sheehy	Table 1.1: 179 Table 2.3: 134 Table 5.1: 179 Table 5.3: —
Nebraska	Kenneth Stephan	Table 2.1: — Table 2.3: — Table 5.1: 208 Table 5.3: 130
New Mexico	Richard Bosson	Table 2.1: — Table 2.3: — Table 5.1: 312 Table 5.3: 180
North Carolina	Paul Martin Newby Sam Ervin	Table 1.1: 966 Table 2.3: 668 Table 5.1: 966 Table 5.3: —
Ohio	Robert Cupp William O'Neill	Table 1.1: 354 Table 2.3: 242 Table 5.1: 354 Table 5.3: —

STATE	CANDIDATES	NUMBER OF RESPONDENTS IN DIFFERENT ANALYSES
Ohio	Yvette McGee Brown Sharon Kennedy	Table 1.1: 412 Table 2.3: 285 Table 5.1: 412 Table 5.3: —
Ohio	Terrence O'Donnell Michael Skindell	Table 1.1: 383 Table 2.3: 249 Table 5.1: 383 Table 5.3: —
Oklahoma	James Edmondson	Table 1.1: — Table 2.3: — Table 5.1: 55 Table 5.3: 40
Oklahoma	Yvonne Kauger	Table 1.1: — Table 2.3: — Table 5.1: 55 Table 5.3: 43
Oklahoma	Douglas Combs	Table 2.1: — Table 2.3: — Table 5.1: 60 Table 5.3: 41
Oklahoma	Norma Gurich	Table 1.1: — Table 2.3: — Table 5.1: 68 Table 5.3: 50
Oklahoma	Arlene Johnson	Table 1.1: — Table 2.3: — Table 5.1: 74 Table 5.3: 45
Oklahoma	David Lewis	Table 1.1: — Table 2.3: — Table 5.1: 69 Table 5.3: 40
Oklahoma	Carlene Clancy Smith	Table 1.1: — Table 2.3: — Table 5.1: 75 Table 5.3: 58
Oregon	Richard Baldwin Nena Cook	Table 1.1: 686 Table 2.3: — Table 5.1: 686 Table 5.3: —

STATE	CANDIDATES	NUMBER OF RESPONDENTS IN DIFFERENT ANALYSES
South Dakota	Glen Severson	Table 1.1: — Table 2.3: — Table 5.1: 125 Table 5.3: 81
Texas	Nathan Hecht Michele Petty Jim Chisholm Mark Ash	Table 1.1: 1078 Table 2.3: 720 Table 6.1: 1078 Table 6.3: —
Texas	Sharon Keller Keith Hampton Lance Stott	Table 1.1: 1116 Table 2.3: 787 Table 5.1: 1116 Table 5.3: —
Washington	Sheryl Gordon McCloud Richard Sanders	Table 1.1: 826 Table 2.3: 628 Table 5.1: 826 Table 5.3: —
West Virginia	Letitia Chafin Allen Loughry Robin Jean Davis John Yoder	Table 1.1: 245 Table 2.3: — Table 5.1: 245 Table 5.3: —

APPENDIX C: EXPERIMENTS

Experiment 1 (Strong Partisan Information), Chapter 3

PARTISAN AND NONPARTISAN CONDITIONS

Italicized language appears only in the partisan condition.

Judge Michael N. Watkins received his law degree from Yale Law School in 1989. Following law school, Judge Watkins completed a judicial clerkship with the Honorable David K. Winder of the United States District Court, and currently serves as a state district court judge. *As a Republican* Judge Watkins believes judges should interpret the law rather than legislate from the bench. He supports the death penalty, and believes in traditional family values. Judge Watkins thinks state courts should limit abortions. He firmly believes that longer sentencing for criminals is the best way to make them pay their debt to society, and won't let criminals off on legal technicalities.

Judge Marcus T. Simmons was appointed to the state supreme court in 2008 to fill out the final two years of former state supreme court judge Donna Howard, who retired. Judge Simmons, a graduate of Duke Law School, is now seeking election to his own full term on the state Supreme Court. *As a Democrat* Judge Simmons believes judges should use the power of the judiciary to promote equality and fairness in society. He is strongly committed to individual rights, including the right to have an abortion and the rights of same-sex couples to marry. He also thinks that protecting the rights of accused criminals is just as important as protecting the rights of crime victims.

PROTOCOL

Subjects were recruited in two separate experiments, one held in an introductory political science class on October 17, 2011; the second in an introductory economics class held on November 3, 2011. There is no significant difference between the results for the political science class and the economics class, probably due to the fact that most of the students in these classes are taking them to fulfill general education requirements and are not majors in political science. Participation was strictly voluntary, and no incentives were offered for participation, but about 99% of the students chose to participate.

Although compensation is vital to some experiments, particularly those that involve incentivizing certain behaviors or rewarding strong performance, in this instance noncompensation poses no threat to the validity of the experiment for several reasons. First, since only one or two students in each class chose not to participate, the magnitude of any effect from their nonparticipation would be very small. Second, because treatment assignment took place after recruitment, we still have the strong integrity of having the only difference between our groups be due to random chance. Finally, we believe that the nature of voluntary participation without compensation best reflects the real-world nature of citizens' choices to vote because the chances of deriving policy benefits attributable to their individual vote are essentially zero (Riker and Ordeshook 1968).

Subjects were assigned by a random draw into either the partisan or nonpartisan treatment conditions. Students were seated and instructed not to talk to one another while completing their questionnaires (compliance on this request was very good). Students then returned their questionnaires and were subsequently dismissed.

Experiment 2 (Subtle Partisan Information), Chapter 3

PARTISAN AND NONPARTISAN CONDITIONS WITH IDEOLOGICAL CONTENT

Italicized language appears only in the partisan condition.

Judge Michael N. Watkins received his law degree from Yale Law School in 1989. Following law school, Judge Watkins completed a judicial clerkship with the Honorable David K. Winder of the United States District Court, and currently serves as a state district court judge. *As a Republican,* Judge Watkins believes judges should interpret the law rather than legislate from the bench.

Judge Marcus T. Simmons was appointed to the state supreme court in 2008 to fill out the final two years of former state supreme court judge Donna Howard, who retired. Judge Simmons, a graduate of Duke Law School, is now seeking election to his own full term on the state Supreme Court. *As a Democrat,* Judge Simmons believes judges should use the power of the judiciary to promote equality and fairness in society.

PARTISAN AND NONPARTISAN CONDITIONS WITH NO IDEOLOGICAL CONTENT

Italicized language appears only in the partisan condition.

Judge Michael N. Watkins received his law degree from Yale Law School in 1989. Following law school, Judge Watkins completed a judicial clerkship with the Honorable David K. Winder of the United States District Court, and currently serves as a state district court judge. *As a Republican,* Judge Watkins promises to decide cases fairly and behave with integrity.

Judge Marcus T. Simmons was appointed to the state supreme court in 2008 to fill out the final two years of former state supreme court judge Donna Howard, who retired. Judge Simmons, a graduate of Duke Law School, is now seeking election to his own full term on the state Supreme Court. *As a Democrat,* Judge Simmons promises to treat all who come before him equally and behave professionally.

PROTOCOL

Subjects for experiment 2 were recruited in a single experiment in a large general education class on November 14, 2013. To maximize comparability to experiment 1, we used a very similar structure for conducting the experiment. Participation was again strictly voluntary with no material incentives offered for participation. As with experiment 1, nearly all students in attendance participated.

Students were seated at the beginning of class, briefed on the study, and advised that their participation was voluntary. Subjects were assigned by a random draw into one of the four treatment conditions. Students were instructed not to talk to one another until they had completed their questionnaires. Students then returned their questionnaires and completed the remainder of their instructional period as usual.

Experiment 3, Chapter 4

PARTISAN ELECTION CONDITION WITH ELECTED INCUMBENT

Italicized language appears only in the treatment where incumbency is listed on the ballot.

Michael N. Watkins received his law degree from Yale Law School in 1989. Following law school, Judge Watkins completed a judicial clerkship with the Honorable David Winder of the United States District Court. Judge Watkins was elected to the state supreme court in 2006 and is seeking reelection this year. As a Republican, Judge Watkins believes judges should interpret the law rather than legislate from the bench.

Marcus T. Simmons, a graduate of Harvard Law School, previously clerked for Judge Heather Rice of the United States District Court. Judge Simmons was elected to the state's trial court in 2010 and now seeks a position on the state supreme court. As a Democrat, Judge Simmons believes judges should use the power of the judiciary to promote equality and fairness in society.

BALLOT QUESTION. If you had the opportunity to vote in the state supreme court race between Michael N. Watkins and Marcus T. Simmons, would you vote for

—Republican Michael N. Watkins, *the incumbent*
—Democrat Marcus T. Simmons
—I would not vote in this race

NONPARTISAN ELECTION CONDITION WITH ELECTED INCUMBENT

Italicized language appears only in the treatment where incumbency is listed on the ballot.

Michael N. Watkins received his law degree from Yale Law School in 1989. Following law school, Judge Watkins completed a judicial clerkship with the Honorable David Winder of the United States District Court. Judge Watkins was elected to the state supreme court in 2006 and is seeking reelection this year. Judge Watkins believes judges should interpret the law rather than legislate from the bench.

Marcus T. Simmons, a graduate of Harvard Law School, previously clerked for Judge Heather Rice of the United States District Court. Judge Simmons was elected to the state's trial court in 2010 and now seeks a position on the state supreme court. Judge Simmons believes judges should use the power of the judiciary to promote equality and fairness in society.

BALLOT QUESTION. If you had the opportunity to vote in the state supreme court race between Michael N. Watkins and Marcus T. Simmons, would you vote for
—Michael N. Watkins, *the incumbent*
—Marcus T. Simmons
—I would not vote in this race

PARTISAN ELECTION CONDITION WITH APPOINTED INCUMBENT

Italicized language appears only in the treatment where incumbency is listed on the ballot.

Michael N. Watkins received his law degree from Yale Law School in 1989. Following law school, Judge Watkins completed a judicial clerkship with the Honorable David Winder of the United States District Court. Judge Watkins was appointed to the state supreme court in 2010 to finish the term of a retiring judge and is seeking his own full term this year. As a Republican, Judge Watkins believes judges should interpret the law rather than legislate from the bench.

Marcus T. Simmons, a graduate of Harvard Law School, previously clerked for Judge Heather Rice of the United States District Court. Judge Simmons was elected to the state's trial court in 2010 and now seeks a position on the state supreme court. As a Democrat, Judge Simmons believes judges should use the power of the judiciary to promote equality and fairness in society.

BALLOT QUESTION. If you had the opportunity to vote in the state supreme court race between Michael N. Watkins and Marcus T. Simmons, would you vote for

—Republican Michael N. Watkins, *the incumbent*
—Democrat Marcus T. Simmons
—I would not vote in this race

NONPARTISAN ELECTION CONDITION WITH APPOINTED INCUMBENT

Italicized language appears only in the treatment where incumbency is listed on the ballot.

Michael N. Watkins received his law degree from Yale Law School in 1989. Following law school, Judge Watkins completed a judicial clerkship with the Honorable David Winder of the United States District Court. Judge Watkins was appointed to the state supreme court in 2010 to finish the term of a retiring judge and is seeking his own full term this year. As a Republican, Judge Watkins believes judges should interpret the law rather than legislate from the bench.

Marcus T. Simmons, a graduate of Harvard Law School, previously clerked for Judge Heather Rice of the United States District Court. Judge Simmons was elected to the state's trial court in 2010 and now seeks a position on the state supreme court. As a Democrat, Judge Simmons believes judges should use the power of the judiciary to promote equality and fairness in society.

BALLOT QUESTION. If you had the opportunity to vote in the state supreme court race between Michael N. Watkins and Marcus T. Simmons, would you vote for

—Michael N. Watkins, *the incumbent*
—Marcus T. Simmons
—I would not vote in this race

PROTOCOL

Subjects for Experiment 3 were recruited in two waves. In one wave, a sample of undergraduate students from a western university was drawn from a large general education class. Students in the class were drawn from a wide variety of majors with only a limited number of political science majors. The experiment was conducted March 19, 2013. Virtually all students invited to participate in the survey experiment chose to do so. These students received a brief explanation of the nature of the study (that we were interested in learning about how people choose between candidates) but were not told that we were manipulating incumbency as a factor in the vignettes. Subjects were assigned by a random draw into one of the four treatment conditions. Students were instructed not to talk to one another until they had completed their questionnaires, a request with which there was compliance. Students then returned their questionnaires and completed the remainder of their instructional period as usual.

Subjects for the second wave were recruited through Amazon's Mechanical Turk (mTurk) service. Subjects completed the identical survey as the university sample, but they completed their survey online in the popular Qualtrics survey suite. Subjects were randomly assigned using the randomization features of the Qualtics software. These subjects were paid $0.50 to compensate them for their time in participating in the survey.

NOTES

Introduction

1. While we generally classify these states as partisan, in our analysis we code the actual race. Thus, some races in these states might be classified as partisan, while others might be classified as retention, depending on the specifics of each individual race.
2. There may be more examples of this coding in the academic literature; unfortunately, however, most studies are not transparent with how Michigan and Ohio are coded. Thus, it is not always possible to ascertain the coding scheme of the authors, though most scholars appear to code these states as nonpartisan states. Additionally, Michigan and Ohio are commonly coded as partisan by groups (such as the American Judicature Society and Justice at Stake) that are committed to the eradication of judicial elections.
3. Pennsylvania also has multiseat elections, but these seldom occur since there must be two open seats to be filled via partisan election. This last happened in 2007 (and prior to that in 1995 and 1981).
4. In a further wrinkle, Nebraska retains associate justices in districts but elects its chief justice in a statewide election.
5. Peters (2009, 25) examines the code of judicial ethics more broadly and concludes, "state canons of ethics shield incumbents from challengers in the general election, suggesting that they inhibit electoral accountability." Thus, eliminating these codes of ethics might lead to more electoral competition.
6. In an interesting footnote to this case, upon remand and with only one of the original judges deciding the case (due to recusals, resignation, and death), the West Virginia Supreme Court again overturned the trial court's verdict and damages by a 4–1 vote. That is, Massey Energy ultimately prevailed on the merits of the case.

7. Other states (New Mexico, Wisconsin, and West Virginia) followed North Carolina's lead and adopted similar plans (Gaylord 2011).

1 Individual-Level Factors and Voter Participation in State Supreme Court Elections

1. We experimented with including variables in our statistical models below that would account for the presence of a straight-ticket voting option (STVO) in partisan elections and an STVO in quasi-partisan or nonpartisan elections. However, in 2010 all of our partisan states happened to be STVO states, and in 2012 all of our partisan states except for Illinois were STVO states. This limited variability prevented us from replicating the Bonneau and Loepp (2014) results using individual-level data.
2. Illinois requires judges to receive 60% of the vote; New Mexico requires 57%.
3. We use the validated measure of CCES turnout (Ansolabehere and Hersh 2012). The CCES validates general turnout but does not validate in which specific races individuals voted, and this leaves some risk that even if someone accurately reported that they turned out, they could have lied about whether they rolled off on judicial elections. To bolster our confidence that misreporting on roll-off was low among individuals who were verified to have turned out, we compared actual levels of roll-off from official returns in two states, Texas and North Carolina, that have large enough sample sizes to permit us to make inferences to the population from our sample, with levels of roll-off observed in the 2012 CCES. In Texas the two races (Keller vs. Hampton and Petty vs. Hecht) had CCES-reported roll-off of 4.7% and 4.4%, respectively, compared to actual levels of roll-off of 4.0% and 3.9%, respectively. In North Carolina, the slippage was somewhat greater, with observed roll-off of 21.9% while our CCES results found 13.4%. While there is some amount of inevitable error in self-reported measures, we are pleased that the amount of error appears to be relatively modest.
4. Validation was completed by consulting state election records and by CCES project staff. We must concede, though, that while voter turnout for up-ballot offices is validated for accuracy, we do not have validation of whether the voter actually participated in the judicial election. Still, we suspect that the greatest amount of self-reported error in turnout is in the propensity to misreport turnout generally rather than to misreport whether one rolled-off in a judicial election.
5. We use the 2008 MPI for both the 2010 and 2012 judicial election cycles. The MPI is calculated in part on presidential outcome data, and 2008 is the last presidential year for which it is calculated. While in some ways this is not ideal, the MPI does not change much over a four-year period. Moreover, we cannot use the 2012 MPI for the 2012 data because we would be predicting election results on the basis of other election results that were not known at the time of the election.
6. We take up the distinction between the performance of incumbents who are

formally identified as such on the ballot and those incumbents who are not in chapter 4.

7. We note that the 2010 and 2012 results conflict on several points. Where such conflicts exist, we generally have more confidence in the 2012 results given the much larger sample size. Specifically, for home ownership in the roll-off equation, the effects are marginally significant in 2012 but not in 2010. For this variable, the issue is likely one of statistical power—a bigger sample size in 2010 may have yielded significant results. For incumbency, the effect in 2010 is actually of the opposite sign than in 2012, although it is not statistically significant (and thus not different from zero). For race-specific characteristics such as campaign spending, challenger quality, and incumbency, we suspect that the generation of additional data over time where we observe both individual level data and race-specific attributes will be important for a better understanding of these phenomena. Finally, union membership in 2010 seems to increase roll-off rather than decrease it; the effect is even statistically significant. Again, given the dramatic differences in sample size, we have greater confidence in the 2012 results but concede that it is possible that differences in the candidate pools across the two election cycles could also influence these results (e.g., union endorsements in one year but not in the other), and a definitive resolution of the issue may require observing additional data.

2 Vote Choice in State Supreme Court Elections

1. It is worth noting that neither of these arguments appears to have empirical merit. Glick and Emmert (1987), Bonneau (2001), and Hurwitz and Lanier (2003) all find no differences in the quality of judges between alternative selection systems. Also, Hall (2001) finds that, in the aggregate, nonpartisan elections are driven by political factors, just like partisan elections.
2. See appendix A for a description of the CCES and its methodology.
3. More specifically, we used data from eighteen elections in 2010 instead of the seventeen here because Michigan held an election in a multiseat race (two seats were up for election, and voters were allowed to vote for two candidates). In chapter 1, we coded participation in that race and were able to easily incorporate it into the analysis. Unfortunately, in this chapter, incorporating a multiseat race into the analysis would require a fundamentally different approach, leading us to exclude Michigan from the 2010 data, leaving us with only seventeen races. In the 2012 data, we had twenty races to use in our turnout analysis, but both Michigan and West Virginia had multiseat elections and had to be excluded from the analysis in this chapter. Michigan also had one seat that was elected in a single-seat race; that race is included in our analysis. As previously, we do not include races that are not contested by two major party candidates. This includes situations where a major party candidate is opposed only by one or more minor party or independent candidates. In this chapter, we must also exclude four races from 2012 (three from

Minnesota and one from Oregon) where both candidates were from the same party. This is an unusually high number of same-party elections for a single year, and most of these same-party races were rather uncompetitive, as were the races with one major party candidate running against only third-party candidates. Finally, we add that our goal is to study outcomes in general elections, so we focus exclusively on general election outcomes. Only the 2012 race in Georgia went to a run-off election. For the Georgia race (which we included), we simply coded the three major party candidates by their party ID and evaluated vote choice in the general election on the basis of partisanship.

4. Ohio is treated as a nonpartisan state because voters do not see the party affiliation of the candidates on the ballot.
5. We note, though, that Dubois (1980) identified at least some nonpartisan candidates as having partisan linkages in his pioneering study covering elections in the 1948–74 time period.
6. Individuals who voted for nonmajor party candidates are excluded from the analysis.
7. Related to incumbency is the concept of challenger quality. Given our use of challenger quality in chapter 1, its omission from the model in this chapter may seem odd. In models not reported here, we included challenger quality (–1 = Republican quality challenger, 0 = no quality challenger, 1 = Democrat quality challenger) and its interaction with election format. However, in the 2012 data in the subset of partisan elections, incumbency and challenger quality happened to be perfectly collinear, making the model inestimable. In the 2010 data the collinearity is not perfect, but it is quite high. Still wanting to estimate models using challenger quality, we estimated the models using challenger quality alone without interacting it with the election format. In these models the effect of challenger quality was insignificant in the 2010 data and significant and positive in the 2012 data. Across both sets of CCES data, though, the fundamental finding that there are high levels of partisan voting in both partisan and nonpartisan elections is robust to inclusion of challenger quality as a covariate.
8. Specifically, we simulate one thousand draws from a multivariate normal distribution with means equal to a vector of the observed coefficient estimates from the model in Table 2.4 and variances derived from the estimated variance-covariance matrix from that same model. Using these simulated parameters we can then compute the difference in discrete changes in predicted probabilities with appropriate measures of uncertainty. The predicted probabilities on which the differences in discrete changes are calculated are based on the same scenario described above, which means varying partisanship, election format, and spending in a race with no incumbent and all other values held constant at their modal values.
9. We repeated the test described in this section using several different high and low values that were near the maximum and minimum and found that the basic result was not sensitive to the selection of the minimum and maximum values.

3 Voting Decisions in Partisan and Nonpartisan Elections

1. The political science course was composed almost entirely of non–political science majors who were simply taking the course to fulfill a general education requirement, meaning that the students were not likely to be unusually politically sophisticated. To make sure that the students in the political science class were not uniquely good at applying their partisanship to their vote choice in nonpartisan elections, we reran the model interacting enrollment in the political science course with the interaction between partisan format and party identification (a three-way interaction) and all interactions among the constituent terms. This effectively allows us to test the hypothesis that the relationships between partisanship and vote choice (conditional on election format) are themselves conditional on whether the subjects were enrolled in the political science class. The results show that the interaction is not significant and that the relationships between partisanship and vote choice (and the extent to which they are conditioned by election format) are not conditional on whether the subjects were enrolled in the political science class. This finding, along with the observational data presented in the previous chapter, mitigates concerns that this portion of the experimental sample was unusually adept at determining party identification from the statements in the candidate biographies.
2. The following are examples of campaign materials or endorsements that reflect the type of information that circulates in a nominally nonpartisan judicial campaign: For Republicans, consider Nels Swandal's endorsement from the Tea Party and his ad regarding values and not "legislating from the bench"; Tim Tingelstad's campaign site showcasing rhetoric on values and religion; and Tom Christensen's website on which he committed to "deciding cases based on the constitution, statute and precedent not legislating from the bench." For Democrats, consider Carol Hunstein's endorsement from Democratic congressman John Lewis declaring that Hunstein "has shown a true commitment to equality for all Georgians"; JoAnne Kloppenberg's statement about fair procedures for the criminally accused; Planned Parenthood of Montana's endorsement of Beth Baker; and Tim Fox's vote to overturn an Arkansas law banning gay and lesbian couples from adopting. Unfortunately, these materials are no longer available online, but similar examples will no doubt be found in current and future races.
3. As a test to ensure successful randomization, we assessed the relative gender and partisan compositions of the two treatment conditions (partisan versus nonpartisan format). If randomization was successful, the gender and partisan composition of the two conditions should differ only by chance. Results show that we fail to reject the null hypothesis that gender and treatment condition assignment are independent $\chi^2 = 0.42$, $p = 0.517$); the test also suggests that party identification and treatment condition assignment are independent ($\chi^2 = 1.30$, $p = 0.521$).
4. Following the convention shown to be most appropriate by Keith et al.

(1992), we code independent "leaners" as partisans. Coding partisanship in a single variable with the values we use is equivalent to using two dummy variables that are constrained to have the same effect but with opposite signs. The results are substantively similar if independents are dropped from the analysis and we compare only Republicans and Democrats.

4 Does One Good Term Deserve Another?

1. This relatively high defeat rate may reflect the shift from Democratic to Republican control that occurred in partisan election states in the South (Alabama, North Carolina, and Texas) (Kritzer 2011).
2. States that list incumbency on the ballot are Arkansas, Georgia, Idaho, Michigan, Minnesota, and Oregon.
3. See Berinsky, Huber, and Lenz (2012) and Horton, Rand, and Zeckhauser (2011) for a discussion of mTurk and its validity.
4. Specifically, we note that there are some potential issues with the use of the chi-square statistic when cell frequencies are so small. However, the difference of proportions test remains valid.
5. Throughout this volume we have emphasized the value of individual-level data in studying judicial elections, so our choice of aggregate data for this particular test may seem unusual. We would have preferred to use individual-level CCES data for this test, but in the 2012 judicial elections, of the single-member district election states that list incumbency on the ballot, only Oregon and Minnesota had contested judicial elections, and those elections were between members of the same party, making it difficult to determine how to incorporate partisanship. In the 2010 elections, all of the single-member district election states that list incumbency on the ballot were nonpartisan states. We re-estimated several models of vote choice from chapter 2 but excluded partisan election states and included an indicator of whether incumbency was listed on the ballot and the interaction of incumbency and whether incumbency was listed on the ballot. This interaction allows us to determine whether the effect of incumbency is greater when it is specifically indicated on the ballot. The interaction was not statistically significant, supporting the other results in this chapter. While incumbency may be an advantage for candidates, the advantage does not stem from having incumbency listed on the ballot.
6. Consistent with our practice earlier in the book, we only consider a race to be contested if there is a candidate from both major parties. The population of these 166 contested races includes elections held in single-seat districts in Alabama, Arkansas, Georgia, Idaho, Kentucky, Louisiana, Michigan, Minnesota, Mississippi, Montana, Nevada, New Mexico, North Carolina, Ohio, Oregon, Texas, Washington, West Virginia, and Wisconsin. All elections considered here include an incumbent; open-seat elections are not included. While the years selected here run only through 2004, our sample includes many elections from years recent enough to be marked by the television advertising and heavy spending that characterizes recent judicial elections.

7. One might posit that the incumbency cue on the ballot may matter more in nonpartisan elections, where it is the only ballot cue, than in partisan elections. To test for this possibility, we reran the model in table 4.6 using only nonpartisan elections and found the coefficient for whether incumbency is formally listed on the ballot to be statistically insignificant. Thus, even in nonpartisan elections a formal indicator of incumbency on the ballot appears to offer no statistically significant benefit to incumbents.

5 Voting Yes

1. In Illinois, New Mexico, and Pennsylvania, judges are initially selected in partisan elections but keep their jobs in retention elections. In Montana, judges run in nonpartisan elections unless they are unopposed, in which case the election reverts to a retention election. Our discussion in this chapter encompasses all retention elections, regardless of how the judge initially attained his or her seat.
2. Aspin (2011) also finds that higher voter participation is associated in part with an organized opposition to unseat judges, but that organized opposition is neither a necessary nor a sufficient condition for voter participation.
3. In chapter 2, we argued that voters in nonpartisan elections can generally discern the partisanship of the candidates, leading to high rates of partisan voting in nonpartisan elections. This claim may seem, on face, to contradict the claim we advance here that the lack of partisan labels in nonpartisan elections depresses turnout. Our contention is that voters who are unable to infer partisanship in nonpartisan elections will often not participate. The reduced pool of voters in nonpartisan elections is a group of individuals who, for whatever reason, was able to discern partisanship or other ideological cues about the candidates and bring that information to bear on their vote choice in the nominally nonpartisan election. This line of reasoning explains how it is possible for nonpartisan elections have reduced participation (due to lack of information) while we still observe significant use of partisan or ideological criteria among those who do participate in nonpartisan elections.
4. We do not include challenger quality in this model because retention elections have no challengers. We omit incumbency from this model because all judges up for retention are incumbents. Similarly, because retention judges rarely raise or spend funds (Florida and Iowa being the only meaningful exceptions in 2012), we omit per capita spending as well. Including these variables induces intolerably high levels of collinearity with the selection system variables and makes parameter estimation unreliable.
5. Note that these predicted probabilities will be somewhat different than actual rates of roll-off because they represent a scenario where roll-off may be more or less likely than alternative combinations of values. Nevertheless, the differences between the categories are representative of the magnitude of the shifts in roll-off due to a change in selection system.
6. We also note that instead of initial appointment by a governor, in Illinois, Pennsylvania, and New Mexico judges face an initial partisan election before

being subjected to regular retention elections. In these cases, partisanship is inferred from the initial campaign rather than the party of the appointing governor.

7. If only one candidate was facing retention, all respondents in that state were asked about that candidate.
8. We ascertain candidate partisanship in a manner similar to that described in chapter 1, with the primary emphasis being on the party of the appointing governor, but with other factors (especially the candidates' partisanship as declared in their first partisan election in New Mexico, Illinois, and Pennsylvania, or other service in elected or appointed office) considered where relevant.
9. Respondent race and gender are coded using the same scheme as the candidates.

Conclusion

1. All states allow for nonlawyer members of these commissions, and most states require such participation. However, these members are still selected by legal and political elites; the public has no say in who gets on these commissions. Additionally, simply having nonlawyers on the commission does not mean these nonlawyers are representative of the public. For example, they could be dominated by individuals with higher levels of education, income, etc.
2. Recall that judges in Pennsylvania are initially selected in partisan elections but retain their jobs every ten years in retention elections.

REFERENCES

Abramowitz, Alan I., and Kyle Saunders. 1998. "Ideological Realignment in the American Electorate." *Journal of Politics* 60: 634–52.

Abramowitz, Alan I., and Jeffrey A. Segal. 1992. *Senate Elections*. Ann Arbor: University of Michigan Press.

Adamany, David, and Philip Dubois. 1976. "Electing State Judges." *Wisconsin Law Review* 1976: 731–79.

Adrian, Charles R. 1959. "A Typology for Nonpartisan Elections." *Western Political Quarterly* 12: 449–58.

Ai, Chunrong, and Edward C. Norton. 2003. "Interaction Terms in Logit and Probit Models." *Economics Letters* 80: 123–29.

Aldrich, John H. 1995. *Why Parties? The Origin and Transformation of Political Parties in America.* Chicago: University of Chicago Press.

Alvarez, R. Michael, and Jonathan Nagler. 1995. "Economics, Issues and the Perot Candidacy: Voter Choice in the 1992 Presidential Election." *American Journal of Political Science* 39: 714–44.

American Political Science Association. 1950. "Toward a More Responsible Two-Party System: A Report of the Committee on Political Parties." *American Political Science Review* 44: 1–96.

Ansolabehere, Stephen, and Eitan Hersh. 2012. "Validation: What Big Data Reveal about Survey Misreporting and the Real Electorate." *Political Analysis* 20: 437–59.

Ansolabehere, Stephen, Nathaniel Persily, and Charles Stewart III. 2010. "Race, Region, and Vote Choice in the 2008 Election: Implications for the Future of the Voting Rights Act." *Harvard Law Review* 123: 1385–436.

Ansolabehere, Stephen, and Stephen Pettigrew. 2013. "The Electoral Value of Seniority: Does Incumbent Tenure Affect the Attitudes of Voters?" Paper presented at the Midwest Political Science Association Meetings, Chicago.

Ansolabehere, Stephen, and Brian Schaffner. 2011. "Re-Examining the Validity of Different Survey Modes for Measuring Public Opinion in the U.S.: Findings from a 2010 Multi-Mode Comparison." Paper presented at the 2011 CCES Conference, Sundance, UT.

Arbour, Brian K., and Mark J. McKenzie. 2010. "Has the 'New Style' of Judicial Campaigning Reached Lower Court Elections?" *Judicature* 93: 150–60.

———. 2011. "Campaign Messages in Lower-Court Elections after *Republican Party of Minnesota vs. White*." *Justice System Journal* 32: 1–23.

Arizona Free Enterprise Club's Freedom Club PAC v. Bennett (564 US ______), 2011.

Aspin, Larry. 2011. "The 2010 Judicial Retention Elections in Perspective: Continuity and Change from 1964 and 2010." *Judicature* 94: 218–32.

———. 2013. Personal communication on file with author.

Associated Press. 2013. "Lawmakers Study Judicial Selection Methods." *Muskogee Phoenix,* October 31, 2013.

Bannon, Alicia, Eric Velasco, Linda Casey, and Lianna Reagan. 2013. *The New Politics of Judicial Elections, 2011–12: How New Waves of Special Interest Spending Raised the Stakes for Fair Courts.* New York: Brennan Center for Justice.

Barber, Kathleen L. 1971. "Ohio Judicial Elections—Nonpartisan Premises with Partisan Results." *Ohio State Law Journal* 32: 762–89.

Baum, Lawrence. 2003. "Judicial Elections and Judicial Independence: The Voter's Perspective." *Ohio State University Law Journal* 64: 13–41.

Baum, Lawrence, and David Klein. 2007. "Voter Responses to High-Visibility Judicial Campaigns." In Streb, *Running for Judge,* 185–215.

Bend, Doug. 2005. "North Carolina's Public Financing of Judicial Campaigns: A Preliminary Analysis." *Georgetown Journal of Legal Ethics* 18: 597–609.

Benesh, Sara C. 2006. "Understanding Public Confidence in American Courts." *Journal of Politics* 68: 697–707.

Berinsky, Adam J., Gregory A. Huber, and Gabriel S. Lenz. 2012. "Evaluating Online Labor Markets for Experimental Research: Amazon.com's Mechanical Turk." *Political Analysis* 20: 351–68.

Berkowitz, Daniel, and Karen Clay. 2006. "The Effect of Judicial Independence on Courts: Evidence from the American States." *Journal of Legal Studies* 35: 399–440.

Berry, Christopher R., and William G. Howell. 2007. "Accountability and Local Elections: Rethinking Retrospective Voting." *Journal of Politics* 69: 844–58.

Bonneau, Chris W. 2001. "The Composition of State Supreme Courts, 2000." *Judicature* 85: 26–31.

———. 2005. "Electoral Verdicts: Incumbent Defeats in State Supreme Court Elections." *American Politics Research* 33: 818–841.

———. 2007a. "The Dynamics of Campaign Spending in State Supreme Court Elections, 1980–2004." In Streb, *Running for Judge,* 59–72.

———. 2007b. "The Effects of Campaign Spending in State Supreme Court Elections." *Political Research Quarterly* 60: 489–99.

———. 2012. "A Survey of Empirical Evidence Concerning Judicial Elections." *Federalist Society White Paper.* Washington, DC: Federalist Society.

Bonneau, Chris W., and Damon M. Cann. 2011. "Campaign Spending, Diminishing Marginal Returns, and Campaign Finance Restrictions in State Supreme Court Elections." *Journal of Politics* 73: 1267–80.

———. 2012. "Party Identification and Vote Choice in Partisan and Nonpartisan Elections." Paper presented at the 2012 Annual Meeting of the Southern Political Science Association, New Orleans, January 12–14, 2012.

Bonneau, Chris W., and Melinda Gann Hall. 2009. *In Defense of Judicial Elections.* New York: Routledge.

Bonneau, Chris W., Melinda Gann Hall, and Matthew J. Streb. 2011. "*White* Noise: The Unrealized Effects of *Republican Party of Minnesota v. White* on Judicial Elections." *Justice System Journal* 32: 247–68.

Bonneau, Chris W. and, Eric D. Loepp. 2014. "Getting Things Straight: The Effects of Ballot Design and Electoral Structure on Voter Participation." *Electoral Studies* 34: 119–30.

Brace, Paul, Laura Langer, and Melinda Gann Hall. 2001. "Measuring the Preferences of State Supreme Court Judges." *Journal of Politics* 62: 387–413.

Brady, Henry E., Sidney Verba, and Kay Lehman Schlozman. 1995. "Beyond SES: A Resource Model of Political Participation." *American Political Science Review* 89: 271–94.

Brambor, Thomas, William Roberts Clark, and Matt Golder. 2006. "Understanding Interaction Models: Improving Empirical Analyses." *Political Analysis* 14: 63–82.

Brandenburg, Bert. 2014. "Life and Death of Electing Judges." *USA Today,* January 5, 2014.

Brandenburg, Bert, and Rachel Paine Caufield. 2009. "Ardent Advocates." *Judicature* 93: 79–81.

Brown, Adam R. 2013. "Voters Don't Care about Incumbency." Paper presented at the Midwest Political Science Association Conference, Chicago.

Bullock, Charles S., III, and Richard E. Dunn. 1996. "Election Roll-Off: A Test of Three Explanations." *Urban Affairs Review* 32: 71–86.

Burbank, Matthew J. 1997. "Explaining Contextual Effects on Vote Choice." *Political Behavior* 19: 113–32.

Caldeira, Gregory A, Samuel Patterson, and Gregory A. Markko. 1985. "The Mobilization of Voters in Congressional Elections." *Journal of Politics* 47: 490–509.

Campbell, Angus, Philip Converse, Warren Miller, and Donald Stokes. 1960. *The American Voter.* Chicago: University of Chicago Press.

Campbell, James E. 1987. "The Revised Theory of Surge and Decline." *American Journal of Political Science* 31: 965–79.

Campbell, David E., John C. Green, and Geoffrey C. Layman. 2011. "The Party Faithful: Partisan Images, Candidate Religion, and the Electoral Impact of Party Identification." *American Journal of Political Science* 55: 42–58.

Canes-Wrone, Brandice, Tom S. Clark, and Jae-Kwang Park. 2012. "Judicial Independence and Retention Elections." *Journal of Law, Economics, and Organization* 28: 211–34.

Cann, Damon M., and Bryan Cole. 2011. "Does the Electoral College Depress Voter Turnout? Strategic Campaigning, Closeness, and Voter Mobilization in U.S. Presidential Elections." Unpublished manuscript.

Cann, Damon M., and Teena Wilhelm. 2011. "Case Visibility and the Electoral Connection in State Supreme Courts." *American Politics Research* 39: 557–81.

Cann, Damon M., and Jeff Yates. 2008. "Homegrown Institutional Legitimacy: Assessing Citizens' Diffuse Support for State Courts." *American Politics Research* 36: 297–329.

Caperton v. A.T. Massey Coal Co. (556 US 868), 2009.

Carlton, Alfred P. 2003. *Justice in Jeopardy: Reports of the American Bar Association Commission on the 21st Century Judiciary.* Chicago: American Bar Association.

Carpenter, Tim. 2013. "Brownback to Sign Judicial Selection Bill." *Topeka Capital-Journal,* March 26, 2013.

Carroll, Susan J., and Richard L. Fox. 2009. *Gender and Elections: Shaping the Future of American Politics.* 2nd ed. Cambridge: Cambridge University Press.

Caufield, Rachel P. 2007. "The Changing Tone of Judicial Election Campaigns as a Result of *White.*" In Streb, *Running for Judge,* 46–78.

Ceasar, James W., and Robert P. Saldin. 2005. "A New Measure of Party Strength." *Political Research Quarterly* 58: 245–56.

Chertoff, Meryl J. 2010. "Trends in Judicial Selection in the States." *McGeorge Law Review* 42: 47–64.

Chicago Tribune. 2013. "Firing Bad Judges: Two Proposed Amendments Could Give Voters a Fighting Chance." February 24.

Choi, Stephen J., G. Mitu Gulati, and Eric A. Posner. 2010. "Professionals or Politicians: The Uncertain Empirical Case for an Elected Rather Than Appointed Judiciary." *Journal of Law, Economics, and Organization* 26: 290–336.

Citizens United vs. Federal Election Commission (558 US ______), 2010.

Clark, Doug. 2013. "Doug Clark Says Nonpartisan Judicial Elections Help North Carolina." *Winston-Salem Journal,* June 8, 2013. http://www.journalnow.com/opinion/columnists/article_bfda7e2a-cf90–11e2–84e3–0019bb30f31a.html.

Cover, Albert D. 1977. "One Good Term Deserves Another: The Advantage of Incumbency in Congressional Elections." *American Journal of Political Science* 21: 523–41.

Cover, Albert D., and Bruce S. Brumberg. 1982. "Baby Books and Ballots: The Impact of Congressional Mail on Constituent Opinion." *American Journal of Political Science* 76: 347–59.

Cox, Gary W., and Jonathan Katz. 1996. "Why Did the Incumbency Advantage in U.S. House Elections Grow?" *American Journal of Political Science* 40: 478–97.

Cox, Gary, and Michael C. Munger. 1989. "Closeness, Expenditures, and Turnout in the 1982 House Elections." *American Political Science Review* 83: 217–31.

DeSantis, Victor S., and Tari Renner. 1991. "Contemporary Patterns and Trends in Municipal Government Structure." In *The Municipal Yearbook*. Washington, DC: International City/County Management Association.

Dimino, Michael R. 2005. "The Worst Way of Selecting Judges—Except All the Others That Have Been Tried." *Northern Kentucky Law Review* 32: 267–304.

DiPasquale, Denise, and Edward L. Glaeser. 1999. "Incentives and Social Capital: Are Homeowners Better Citizens?" *Journal of Urban Economics* 45: 354–84.

Downs, Anthony. 1957. *An Economic Theory of Democracy*. New York: Harper.

Dubois, Philip L. 1979. "Voter Turnout in State Judicial Elections: An Analysis of the Tail on the Electoral Kite." *Journal of Politics* 41: 865–87.

———. 1980. *From Ballot to Bench: Judicial Elections and the Quest for Accountability*. Austin: University of Texas Press.

Duncan, Samuel John. 1913. *The Progressive Movement: Its Principles and Its Programme*. Boston: Small, Maynard.

Erie Times-News. 2013. "Our View: Merit Selection for Judges Merits Study." April 3.

Fiorina, Morris P. 1977. *Congress: Keystone of the Washington Establishment*. New Haven, CT: Yale University Press.

———. 2002. "Parties and Partisanship: A 40-Year Retrospective." *Political Behavior* 24: 93–115.

Fischer, Howard. 2013. "AZ High Court Nixes Judicial Appointment Process Change." *Maricopa (AZ) Monitor*. September 17, 2013.

Fitzpatrick, Brian T. 2009. "The Politics of Merit Selection." *Missouri Law Review* 74: 675–709.

Fowler, James H. 2008. "The Colbert Bump in Campaign Donations: More Truthful Than Truthy." *PS: Political Science & Politics* 41: 533–39.

Frederick, Brian, and Matthew J. Streb. 2008. "Paying the Price for a Seat on the Bench: Campaign Spending in Contested State Intermediate Appellate Court Elections." *State Politics and Policy Quarterly* 8: 410–29.

———. 2011. "The Cost of Going for the Gavel: Individual Candidate Spending in Intermediate Appellate Court Elections." *Justice System Journal* 32: 25–43.

Freedman, Paul, Michael Franz, and Kenneth Goldstein. 2004. "Campaign Advertising and Democratic Citizenship." *American Journal of Political Science* 48: 723–41.

Gaylord, Scott W. 2011. "Unconventional Wisdom: The Roberts Court's Proper Support of Judicial Elections." *Michigan State Law Review* 2011: 1521–67.

Geyh, Charles Gardner. 2003. "Why Judicial Elections Stink." *Ohio State Law Journal* 64: 43–79.

———. 2005. "The Judgment of the Boss on Bossing the Judges: Bruce Springsteen, Judicial Independence, and the Rule of Law." *Widener Law Journal* 14: 885–905.

———. 2012. "Judicial Selection Reconsidered: A Plea for Radical Moderation." *Harvard Journal of Law and Public Policy* 35: 623–42.

———. 2014. "Judicial Independence as an Organizing Principle." *Annual Review of Law and Social Science*. Forthcoming.

Gibson, James L. 2012. *Electing Judges: The Surprising Effects of Campaigning on Judicial Legitimacy.* Chicago: University of Chicago Press.

Gibson, James L., Jeffrey A. Gottfried, Michael X. Delli Carpini, and Kathleen Hall Jamieson. 2011. "The Effects of Judicial Campaign Activity on the Legitimacy of Courts: A Survey-Based Experiment." *Political Research Quarterly* 64: 545–558.

Gill, Rebecca D. 2013. "Beyond High Hopes and Unmet Expectations: Judicial Selection Reforms in the States." *Judicature* 96: 278–95.

Gill, Rebecca D., Sylvia R. Lazos, and Mallory M. Waters. 2011. "Are Judicial Performance Evaluations Fair to Women and Minorities? A Cautionary Tale from Clark County, Nevada." *Law and Society Review* 45: 731–59.

Glick, Henry R., and Craig F. Emmert. 1987. "Selection Systems and Judicial Characteristics: The Recruitment of State Supreme Court Judges." *Judicature* 70: 228–35.

Goelzhauser, Greg, and Damon M. Cann. 2014. "Judicial Independence and Opinion Clarity in State Supreme Courts." *State Politics and Policy Quarterly* 14: 123–41.

Gould, Lewis L. 1986. *Reform and Regulation: American Politics from Roosevelt to Wilson,* 2nd ed. New York: Knopf.

Gouras, Matt. "Republican Senator Wants to Change Montana Supreme Court Qualifications." *Missoulian* (Missoula, MT), January 24, 2013.

Green, Donald P., and Jonathan S. Krasno. 1988. "Salvation for the Spendthrift Incumbent: Reestimating the Effects of Campaign Spending in House Elections." *American Journal of Political Science* 32: 884–907.

Green, Donald P., Bradley Palmquist, and Eric Schickler. 2002. *Partisan Hearts and Minds: Political Parties and the Social Identity of Voters.* New Haven: Yale University Press.

Hall, Melinda Gann. 1995. "Justices as Representatives: Elections and Judicial Politics in the American States." *American Politics Quarterly* 23: 485–503.

———. 2001. "State Supreme Courts in American Democracy: Probing the Myths of Judicial Reforms." *American Political Science Review* 95: 315–30.

———. 2007. "Voting in State Supreme Court Elections: Competition and Context as Democratic Incentives." *Journal of Politics* 69: 1147–59.

Hall, Melinda Gann, and Chris W. Bonneau. 2006. "Does Quality Matter? Challengers in State Supreme Court Elections." *American Journal of Political Science* 50: 20–33.

———. 2008. "Mobilizing Interest: The Effects of Money on Citizen Participation in State Supreme Court Elections." *American Journal of Political Science* 52: 457–70.

Hanna, John. 2013. "Kansas GOP's Push to Change Judicial Selection Meets Resistance." *Topeka Capital-Journal,* January 27, 2013.

Hasen, Richard L. 2007. "First Amendment Limits on Regulating Judicial Campaigns." In Streb, *Running for Judge,* 20–45.

Helgeson, Baird. 2013. "Political Divide Emerges on Plan to Overhaul Minnesota Judicial Elections." *Minneapolis Star Tribune,* September 22, 2013.

Henderson, John, and Sara Chatfield. 2011. "Who Matches? Propensity Scores and Bias in the Causal Effects of Education on Participation." *Journal of Politics* 73: 646–58.

Highton, Benjamin, and Cindy D. Kam. 2011. "The Long-Term Dynamics of Partisanship and Issue Orientations." *Journal of Politics* 73: 202–15.

Hillygus, D. Sunshine. 2005. "The Missing Link: Exploring the Relationship between Higher Education and Political Engagement." *Political Behavior* 27: 25–47.

Hinich, Melvin J., and Michael Munger. 1997. *Analytical Politics.* New York: Cambridge University Press.

Hofstadter, Richard. 1955. *The Age of Reform: From Bryan to FDR.* New York: Knopf.

Horton, John J., David G. Rand, and Richard J. Zeckhauser. 2011. "The Online Laboratory: Conducting Experiments in a Real Labor Market." *Experimental Economics* 14: 399–425.

Huckfeldt, Robert, Jeffrey Levine, William Morgan, and John Sprague. 1999. "Accessibility and the Political Utility of Partisan and Ideological Orientations." *American Journal of Political Science* 43: 888–911.

Huffstetler, Tripp. 2013. "RIP: The Death of Publicly Funded Judicial Elections in North Carolina." *Campbell Law Observer,* July 31, 2013.

Humphrey, Tom. 2013. "Expiring State Commission Wants to Select Judge Candidates Months Early." *Knoxville News Sentinel.* June 9, 2013.

Hurwitz, Mark S., and Drew Noble Lanier. 2003. "Explaining Judicial Diversity: The Differential Ability of Women and Minorities to Attain Seats on State Supreme and Appellate Courts." *State Politics and Policy Quarterly* 3: 329–52.

Iyengar, Shanto. 2002. "The Effects of Media-Based Campaigns on Candidate and Voter Behavior: Implications for Judicial Elections." *Indiana Law Review* 35: 691–99.

Jacobson, Gary. 2013. *The Politics of Congressional Elections.* 8th ed. New York: Pearson.

Johnson, Charles A., Roger C. Shaefer, and R. Neal McKnight. 1978. "The Salience of Judicial Candidates and Elections." *Social Science Quarterly* 59: 371–78.

Justice at Stake. 2013. "Supreme Court Justice Sandra Day O'Connor Joins Justice at Stake as Honorary Chair." April 15. http://www.justiceatstake.org/newsroom/press-releases-16824/?supreme_court_justice_sandra_day_oconnor_joins_justice_at_stake_as_honorary_chair&show=news&newsID=16396.

Kabler, Phil. 2013. "W.Va. Elections Commission Approves Public Financing Rules." *Charleston Gazette,* May 30, 2013. http://www.wvgazette.com/News/201305300113.

Kam, Cindy D. 2005. "Who Toes the Party Line? Cues, Values, and Individual Differences." *Political Behavior* 27: 163–82.

Kam, Cindy, and Carl Palmer. 2008. "Reconsidering the Effects of Education on Citizen Participation." *Journal of Politics* 70: 612–31.

Keith, Bruce E., David B. Magleby, Candice J. Nelson, Elizabeth A. Orr, Mark C.

Westlye, and Raymond E. Wolfinger. 1992. *The Myth of the Independent Voter.* Berkeley: University of California Press.

Kellstedt, Paul M., and Guy D. Whitten. 2013. *The Fundamentals of Political Science Research.* 2nd ed. New York: Cambridge University Press.

Kenny, Christopher. 1998. "The Behavioral Consequences of Political Discussion: Another Look at Discussant Effects on Vote Choice." *Journal of Politics* 60: 231–44.

King, Gary, Michael Tomz, and Jason Wittenberg. 2000. "Making the Most of Statistical Analyses: Improving Interpretation and Presentation." *American Journal of Political Science* 44: 341–55.

Klein, David, and Lawrence Baum. 2001. "Ballot Information and Voting Decisions in Judicial Elections." *Political Research Quarterly* 54: 709–28.

Kornhauser, Lewis A. 2002. "Is Judicial Independence a Useful Concept?" In *Judicial Independence at the Crossroads: An Interdisciplinary Approach,* edited by Stephen B. Burbank and Barry Friedman, 45–55. Thousand Oaks, CA: Sage.

Krasno, Jonathan S., and Donald P. Green. 2008. "Do Televised Presidential Ads Increase Voter Turnout? Evidence from a Natural Experiment." *Journal of Politics* 70: 245–61.

Kritzer, Herbert M. 2007. "'Law is the Mere Continuation of Politics by Different Means': American Judicial Selection in the Twenty-First Century." *DePaul Law Review* 56: 423–67.

———. 2011. "Competitiveness in State Supreme Court Elections, 1946–2009." *Journal of Empirical Legal Studies* 8: 237–59.

Layman, Geoffrey C. 1997. "Religion and Political Behavior in the United States: The Impact of Beliefs, Affiliations, and Commitment from 1980 to 1994." *Political Opinion Quarterly* 61: 288–316.

Leighley, Jan, and Jonathan Nagler. 2007. "Unions, Voter Turnout, and Class Bias in the Electorate, 1964–2004." *Journal of Politics* 69: 430–41.

Levendusky, Matthew S. 2009. *The Partisan Sort: How Liberals Became Democrats and Conservatives Became Republicans.* Chicago: University of Chicago Press.

Levine, Jeffrey, Edward C. Carmines, and Robert Huckfeldt. 1997. "The Rise of Ideology in the Post–New Deal Party System, 1972–92." *American Politics Quarterly* 25: 19–34.

Margolies, Dan. 2002. "Ruling Throws a Wrench into the Missouri Plan." *Kansas City Star,* July 16, 2002, D18.

Mayhew, David R. 1974. *Congress: The Electoral Connection.* New Haven: Yale University Press.

———. 2008. *Parties and Politics: How the American Government Works.* New Haven: Yale University Press.

McNutt, Michael. 2013. "Survey Shows Support for Electing Oklahoma's Appellate Judges, Justices." *Oklahoman* (Oklahoma City), August 28, 2013.

Mercer, Bob. 2013. "Bill Gives Lawmakers More Say on Judicial Appointments." *Rapid City (SD) Journal,* February 6, 2013.

Milburn, John. 2013. "Kansas Judicial Selection Issue Part of National Trend." *Topeka Capital-Journal,* May, 11, 2013.

Mondics, Chris. 2013. "Pennsylvania Bill Would Change How Judges Are Chosen." *Philadelphia Inquirer,* January 25, 2013.

Morton, Rebecca B., and Kenneth C. Williams. 2010. *Experimental Political Science and the Study of Causality: From Nature to the Lab.* New York: Cambridge University Press.

Moser, Whet. 2013. "As Chicago Judge Goes on Trial, a Proposal to Fix the System That Keeps Bad Judges on the Bench." *Chicago Magazine,* February 4, 2013. http://www.chicagomag.com/Chicago-Magazine/The-312/February-2013/Time-To-Give-Up-on-Elected-Judges-in-Illinois/.

Musgrave, Beth. 2013. "Public Financing of Judicial Elections Passes House." *Bluegrass Politics: Covering Kentucky Politics and Government,* March 4, 2013. http://bluegrasspolitics.bloginky.com/2013/03/04/public-financing-of-judicial-elections-passes-house/.

Nelson, Jennifer. 2013. "Legislation on Judicial Nominating Commission Members Moves to House." *Indiana Lawyer,* February 15, 2013. http://www.theindianalawyer.com/article/print?articleId=30781.

Nelson, Michael J. 2011. "Uncontested and Unaccountable? Rates of Contestation in Trial Court Elections." *Judicature* 94: 208–217.

Nichols, Stephen M., and Gregory A. Strizek. 1995. "Electronic Voting Machines and Ballot Roll-Off." *American Politics Quarterly* 23: 300–318.

North Carolina Voters for Clean Elections. 2012. "NC Judicial Public Financing: A Success Story." http://www.ncvce.org/content/nc-judicial-public-financing-success-story. Accessed on December 20, 2012.

O'Brien, John. 2013. "Legislature Passes Public Financing Bill for SC Elections." *West Virginia Record.* April 15, 2013. http://wvrecord.com/news/259285-legislature-passes-public-financing-bill-for-sc-elections.

O'Connor, Maureen. 2013. "Let's Improve How Judges Are Selected." *Columbus (OH) Dispatch,* May 26, 2013.

O'Connor, Sandra Day, and Ruth V. McGregor. 2012. "Judicial Selection Principles: A Perspective." *Albany Law Review* 75: 1741–46.

Olorunnipa, Toluse, and Brittany Alana Davis. 2012. "Florida Voters Reject Most Constitutional Amendments, Including 'Religious Freedom' Proposal." *Tampa Bay Times,* November 6, 2012.

Olson, Susan M. 2001. "Voter Mobilization in Judicial Retention Elections: Performance Evaluations and Organized Opposition." *Justice System Journal* 22: 263–85.

Ornstein, Norman J., Thomas E. Mann, Michael J. Malbin, and Andrew Rugg. 2013. *Vital Statistics on Congress.* Washington, DC: Brookings Institution.

Page, Benjamin I. and Robert Y. Shapiro. 1992. *The Rational Public: Fifty Years of Trends in Americans' Policy Preferences.* Chicago: University of Chicago Press.

Persily, Nathaniel, and Kelli Lammie. 2004. "Perceptions of Corruption and Campaign Finance: When Public Opinion Determines Constitutional Law." *University of Pennsylvania Law Review* 153: 119–80.

Peters, C. Scott. 2007. "Canons, Cost, and Competition in State Supreme Court Elections." *Judicature* 91: 27–35.

———. 2008. "Campaigning for State Supreme Court, 2006." *Justice System Journal* 29: 166–86.

———. 2009. "Canons of Ethics and Accountability in State Supreme Court Elections." *State Politics and Policy Quarterly* 9: 24–55.

Pomper, Gerald. 1966. "Ethnic and Group Voting in Nonpartisan Municipal Elections." *Public Opinion Quarterly* 30: 79–97.

Pozen, David E. 2008. "The Irony of Judicial Elections." *Columbia Law Review* 108: 265–330.

Rabinowitz, George, Paul-Henri Gurian, and Stuart Elaine Macdonald. 1984. "The Structure of Presidential Elections and the Process of Realignment, 1944 to 1980." *American Journal of Political Science* 28: 611–35.

Raftery, Bill. 2013. "Georgia Bill Would Create A Merit-Selection Style Panel for Interim Vacancies; Gives 18 of 23 Seats to Minority Bar Associations." *Gavel to Gavel: A Review of State Legislation Affecting the Courts.* January 11, 2013. http://gaveltogavel.us/site/2013/01/11/georgia-bill-would-create-a-merit-selection-style-panel-for-interim-vacancies-gives-18-of-23-seats-to-minority-bar-associations/.

Republican Party of Minnesota v. White (536 US 765), 2002.

Riker, William H., and Peter C. Ordeshook. 1968. "A Theory of the Calculus of Voting." *American Political Science Review* 62: 25–42.

Rivers, Douglas. 2007. "Sampling for Web Surveys." Paper presented at the 2007 Joint Statistical Meetings, Salt Lake City, UT. Available on-line at http://www.laits.utexas.edu/txp_media/html/poll/files/Rivers_matching.pdf.

Rock, Emily, and Lawrence Baum. 2010. "The Impact of High-Visibility Contests for U.S. State Court Judgeships: Partisan Voting in Nonpartisan Elections." *State Politics and Policy Quarterly* 10: 368–96.

Rosenstone, Steven J., and John Mark Hansen. 1993. *Mobilization, Participation, and Democracy in America.* Longman: New York.

Savchak, Elisha Carol, and A. J. Barghothi. 2007. "The Influence of Appointment and Retention Constituencies: Testing Strategies of Judicial Decisionmaking." *State Politics and Policy Quarterly* 7: 394–415.

Schaffner, Brian F., Matthew Streb, and Gerald Wright. 2001. "Teams without Uniforms: The Nonpartisan Ballot in State and Local Elections." *Political Research Quarterly* 54: 7–30.

Schattschneider, Elmer E. 1942. *Party Government.* New York: Holt, Rinehart, and Winston.

Schorsch, Peter. 2013. "League of Women Voters Says House Bill Would Undermine Judicial Merit Selection Process." *SaintPetersBlog,* March, 28, 2013. http://www.saintpetersblog.com/league-of-women-voters-says-house-bill-would-undermine-judicial-merit-selection-process.

Schotland, Roy A. 2002. "Should Judges Be More Like Politicians?" *Court Review* 39: 8–11.

———. 2003. "To the Endangered Species List, Add: Nonpartisan Judicial Elections." *Willamette Law Review* 39: 1397–422.

Shaw, Daron, Rodolfo O. de la Garza, and Jongho Lee. 2000. "Examining Latino

Turnout in 1996: A Three-State, Validated Survey Approach." *American Journal of Political Science* 44: 332–40.

Shepsle, Kenneth A. 1978. *The Giant Jigsaw Puzzle: Democratic Committee Assignments in the Modern House.* Chicago: University of Chicago Press.

Shugerman, Jed Handelsman. 2012. *The People's Courts: Pursuing Judicial Independence in America.* Cambridge, MA: Harvard University Press.

Skaggs, Adam, Maria da Silva, Linda Casey, and Charles Hall. 2011. *The New Politics of Judicial Elections, 2009–10.* Washington, DC: Justice at Stake Campaign.

Sondheimer, Rachel Milstein, and Donald P. Green. 2010. "Using Experiments to Estimate the Effects of Education on Voter Turnout." *American Journal of Political Science* 54: 174–89.

Spektor, Andrey, and Michael Zuckerman. 2011. "Judicial Recusal and Expanding Notions of Due Process." *University of Pennsylvania Journal of Constitutional Law* 13: 977–1015.

Squire, Peverill, and Eric R. A. N. Smith. 1988. "The Effect of Partisan Information on Voters in Nonpartisan Elections." *Journal of Politics* 50: 169–79.

Streb, Matthew J., ed. *Running for Judge: The Rising Political, Financial, and Legal Stakes of Judicial Elections.* New York: New York University Press.

Streb, Matthew J., and Brian Frederick. 2009. "Conditions for Competition in Low-Information Judicial Elections: The Case of Intermediate Appellate Court Elections." *Political Research Quarterly* 62: 523–537.

———. 2011. "When Money Cannot Encourage Participation: Campaign Spending and Rolloff in Low Visibility Judicial Elections." *Political Behavior* 33: 665–84.

Streb, Matthew J., Brian Frederick, and Casey LaFrance. 2007. "Contestation, Competition, and the Potential for Accountability in Intermediate Appellate Court Elections." *Judicature* 91: 70–78.

———. 2009. "Voter Rolloff in a Low-Information Context: Evidence from Intermediate Appellate Court Elections." *American Politics Research* 37: 644–69.

Sulzberger, A. G. 2010. "In Iowa, Voters Oust Judges over Marriage Issue." *New York Times,* November 3, 2010.

Timpone, Richard J. 1998. "Structure, Behavior, and Voter Turnout in the United States." *American Political Science Review* 92: 145–58.

Tyler, Tom R. 2000. "Social Justice: Outcome and Procedure." *International Journal of Psychology* 35: 117–25.

Van de Ven, Wynand P. M. M., and Bernard M. S. Van Praag. 1981. "The Demand for Deductibles in Private Health Insurance: A Probit Model with Same Selection." *Journal of Econometrics* 17: 229–52.

WACH FOX. 2013. "Bill Would Expand Lawmakers' Choices for SC Judges." January 25 http://www.wach.com/news/story.aspx?id=852189#.UnkfgZQ-uCg

Williams, Kenneth C. 2013. *Introduction to Game Theory: A Behavioral Approach.* New York: Oxford University Press.

Wolfinger, Raymond E., and Steven J. Rosenstone. 1980. *Who Votes?* New Haven: Yale University Press.

INDEX